WALKING ON
THE ISLE OF WIGHT

About the Author

Paul Curtis left the world of office administration to write this guidebook, having enjoyed writing a popular blog about a 2008 solo cycling trip from Boston to San Diego. He loves travelling, particularly long-distance hiking and cycling, and enjoys getting away to as many wonderful places as possible in his free time. He fell in love with the Isle of Wight on his first visit in 2008, and returned periodically to walk there before making it his home in 2011.

In addition to his US adventure, Paul has cycled from Amsterdam to Sarandë in Albania and from Calais to Istanbul, hiked across Switzerland and has completed several long-distance walking trails in the UK including the North Downs Way, the Thames Path and the Hertfordshire Way. He has designed a South of England figure of eight walk, stretching from Dover to Land's End and centred on Windsor. He is a solo, romantic explorer in the Wainwright tradition and believes that guidebooks should first and foremost be about finding the most beautiful routes and providing precise, accurate descriptions.

Paul lives and works on the Isle of Wight.

WALKING ON
THE ISLE OF WIGHT

by Paul Curtis

2 POLICE SQUARE, MILNTHORPE, CUMBRIA LA7 7PY
www.cicerone.co.uk

© Paul Curtis 2017
Second edition 2017
ISBN: 978 1 85284 873 6
First edition 2013

Printed in China on behalf of Latitude Press Ltd
A catalogue record for this book is available from the British Library.

© Crown copyright OS PU100012932
All photographs are by the author unless otherwise stated.

Acknowledgements

Thanks to the Hampshire and Isle of Wight Wildlife Trust for their advice on the Wildlife section of this guide.

For my friend Ruth

Updates to this Guide

While every effort is made by our authors to ensure the accuracy of guidebooks as they go to print, changes can occur during the lifetime of an edition. Any updates that we know of for this guide will be on the Cicerone website (www.cicerone.co.uk/873/updates), so please check before planning your trip. We also advise that you check information about such things as transport, accommodation and shops locally. Even rights of way can be altered over time. We are always grateful for information about any discrepancies between a guidebook and the facts on the ground, sent by email to updates@cicerone.co.uk or by post to Cicerone, 2 Police Square, Milnthorpe LA7 7PY, United Kingdom.

Front cover: The Needles (Walk 4)

CONTENTS

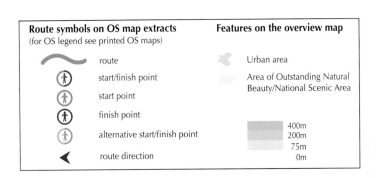

Route symbols on OS map extracts
(for OS legend see printed OS maps)

- route
- start/finish point
- start point
- finish point
- alternative start/finish point
- route direction

Features on the overview map

- Urban area
- Area of Outstanding Natural Beauty/National Scenic Area

400m
200m
75m
0m

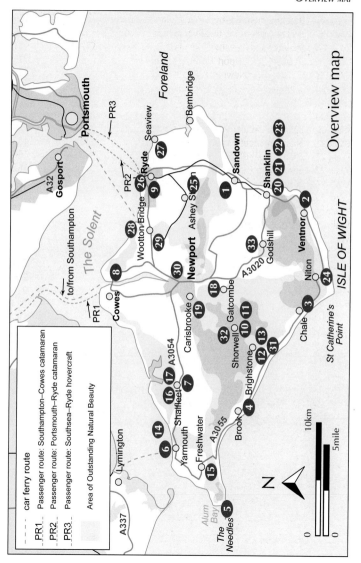

Overview map

Cliffs near Ventnor (Walk 2)

INTRODUCTION

It is surprising that, in spite of the Isle of Wight's beauty and elegance, this peaceful and perfect-sized island is often dismissed simply as a place to go for a long weekend or somewhere to send children on school trips. Perhaps it is because many visitors tend not to penetrate the island beyond the resorts and the tourist attractions. But those with curiosity are likely to fall in love with this place; its variety of scenery and understated aesthetic qualities are appreciated most by those on foot, with almost everywhere being accessible courtesy of the green buses which stand out on the landscape. The Isle of Wight is made for walking!

Nearly half the island is a designated Area of Outstanding Natural Beauty, but this is misleading as almost the entire island can rightly be called beautiful. There are jaw-dropping views such as those from the magnificent coastline of West Wight, St Boniface, Culver and Brading Downs, St Catherine's Point and the Needles. And there is also a gentler, more intimate beauty at countless locations unknown even by many islanders, such as remote Newtown Harbour, an 'undiscovered' balcony trail near Gatcombe, and even the scenic path linking urban Carisbrooke and Newport.

Yaverland cliffs (Walk 9)

The island's default scenery is graceful, undulating downland, very attractive to the eye, and if you walk in any direction for up to 5 miles you would almost certainly glimpse the sea. Tree-lovers are also well catered for, with the large and lonely Brighstone Forest being particularly attractive, situated on top of the magnificent West Wight ridge of downs and offering enchanting sea views from its southern fringe. And sea-lovers will be enamoured with the Coastal Path; simply a stunner! Only thrill-seeking walkers or those not interested in anything except alpine scenery would be disappointed with the Isle of Wight.

There are an incredible 525km (326 miles) of footpaths on an island of just 381 square kilometres (147 square miles), and there are more footpaths and bridleways than roads. Such a choice of where to walk means that walkers can experience all the diversity the island has to offer – not only scenery but also many of the 2000 or so listed buildings – and that the trails are not too crowded, except on very popular routes in high season.

The Isle of Wight is an ideal size for a walking holiday – not so small that visitors can become familiar with it in under a week, yet small enough to walk from Bembridge on the east coast to the Needles on the west coast in a single day. Away from the few towns and sometimes cheesy (yet charming) coastal resorts, the island is genuinely a walker's paradise: an overused term, but definitely applicable in this case. This is not just because of the consistently attractive, varied scenery and preponderance of footpaths, but also because of a particularly mild, temperate climate, exceptionally good access to walks via public transport, and optimum levels of safety – the last of which makes it an especially good destination for beginners and families to try some walking.

The fact that the Isle of Wight is not teeming with walkers all year round is everyone else's loss and your gain.

GEOGRAPHY AND LANDSCAPE

The island is diamond-shaped, about 37km (23 miles) from Bembridge (east) to the Needles (west), and 21km (13 miles) from Cowes (north) to St Catherine's Point (south). This makes it small enough to cross by car in about an hour, but large enough to offer a huge variety of interest in terms of both natural landscape and towns and villages. First-time visitors may be surprised at just how close the mainland seems; from Yarmouth it is only 1.5km (1 mile) away. On clear days and from lofty vantage points, the mainland coastline can be seen as far as Bournemouth and the Isle of Purbeck to the west and Beachy Head to the east – which perhaps contributes to disagreements over whether the island is more a part of southwest or southeast England. But on the south-facing coasts the open sea seems endless; the eye looks towards France but never sees it.

There are eight towns on the island: Yarmouth, Cowes, East Cowes and Ryde on the north coast, the resorts of Sandown, Shanklin and Ventnor on the east coast, and Newport in the centre. The sprawling and ambiguously defined village of Freshwater comprises most of the far west. Unlike many towns on the mainland, each feels unique and has a special character. Villages and hamlets are numerous and all maintain a distinct identity, derived from a sense of location and history; they are much more than their constituent streets and buildings. Some, notably Godshill and Shorwell, are decidedly photogenic, with an abundance of thatched cottages and attractive stone houses.

But it is the downland that really makes the island great, and it is thoroughly explored in these walks. There can be said to be three major stretches: from Newport east to the sea (St George's Down to Culver Down); the 'southeast downs' which form an arc around the village of Wroxall; and from Carisbrooke southwest to the so-called 'Back of the Wight' (the southwest coastline from Chale to Freshwater Bay and the villages just behind). The key to mastering the geography of the island is familiarity with the downs.

The sea around the entire island, both the Solent and English Channel proper, is notoriously rough and has claimed numerous ships and lives. The south is very prone to cliff erosion and landslips because of its secondary layer of gault clay (known as

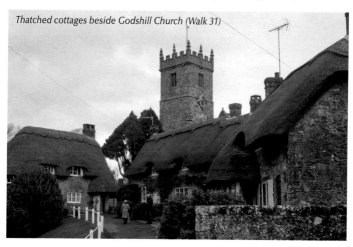

Thatched cottages beside Godshill Church (Walk 31)

'blue slipper'). When rain permeates the gault it moves forward, causing the instability. This process, together with rising sea levels after the last ice age, created the Undercliff between Ventnor and Niton. Today erosion and landslips still cause problems – not least Coastal Path diversions – the island is continually getting smaller. The Blackgang Chine attraction, located on a cliff-top near Niton, has particularly suffered over the years, and in 1928 a major landslip a little to the east caused an irreparable breach in the old Niton to Blackgang road.

But erosion is not all bad. One positive by-product is that it constantly reveals new fossils. The island is nicknamed the 'Dinosaur Isle' because of the large number of fossils that may be found, especially on the beaches at Compton Bay (see Walk 4) and Yaverland (see Walk 9). Along the Back of the Wight, erosion has enlarged several 'chines' (a local term for a breach in a sea-cliff) and created caves, such as those below Tennyson Down.

The north of the island has a firmer geological foundation, its hard clays supporting a surprisingly large and varied range of woodland (some ancient). These include eerie Parkhurst Forest, America Wood and numerous smaller woods, although deforestation has occurred regularly throughout the ages. Much planting of non-native but red-squirrel-friendly trees (such as the Scots pine and the sycamore) has taken place over the past 100 years, but the trend now is to increase the proportion of native species while also increasing biodiversity.

Effects of erosion (Walk 3)

America Wood (Walks 22 and 26)

Unusually, all rivers on the island flow north. The Medina and Western Yar are remarkable for their oversized estuaries (from Newport to Cowes, and Freshwater to Yarmouth respectively). The Eastern Yar flows from Niton to Bembridge, and Newtown River and Wootton Creek are fed by multiple streams.

The National Trust has a very strong presence on the island, owning and maintaining precious areas such as Newtown Harbour and the Needles Batteries, and there are a total of 41 Special Sites of Scientific Interest (SSSIs), which include woods, downs and marshes. All in all, the landscape features of the Isle of Wight are expertly protected, whether by the National Trust, Forestry Commission or the council.

A POTTED HISTORY

There are two principal theories as to the origin of 'Wight'. The root word may have originated in the Iron Age and been subsequently altered many times, including by the Romans who called the island Vectis; the original definition apparently meant 'little appendage'. Another theory is that 'Vectis' is unrelated to previous names, and that the root of the modern name derived from the original name for Carisbrooke: Wihtgarsburh – possibly named after a Saxon king.

For the vast majority of the Earth's history, there was no Isle of Wight as such, as the island we know today was part of the mainland. Dinosaurs arrived some 125 million years ago when the region was then situated near the Equator, and today 'Dinosaur

13

Isle' is world-renowned for its fossils, especially along Compton Bay, the beach at Yaverland and Bouldnor Cliffs. Finds are often not particularly significant – commonly fossilised iguanodon footprints – but skeletons of *Hypsilophodon* and *Neovenator salerii* have been discovered.

It was only during the past 8000–10,000 years that an island was formed, caused by the sea flooding the Solent valley at the end of the last ice age and subsequently eroding the coastlines. In those days, the island was wholly covered by oak and elm, and it was only in about 3000BC that the sedentary agricultural lifestyle started to replace the hunter-gatherer way of life – trees were felled and cereals cultivated, allowing more complex societies to develop on the fledgling island.

Trading routes were soon established over the downs, and today's walkers will be reminded of life in this Neolithic period by communal burial mounds, known as barrows, alongside these routes, notably on the Back of the Wight. The Long Stone near Mottistone is a more tangible ancient monument; it is likely that Neolithic people met here to discuss and debate.

The islanders were no match for the Roman army, which invaded in AD43 led by Vespasian, the future emperor. The island never really flourished under Roman rule; seven or eight villas were built for the wealthy – the ones at Brading and Newport have been preserved and are open to the public – but no towns or roads were constructed as they were on the mainland. However, one industry started during Roman times was to last for centuries: stone quarrying at Binstead. Winchester and Chichester cathedrals, as well as the island's first Quarr Abbey, were built using Binstead stone.

After the Romans left in the fifth century, Saxon King Cerdic conquered the island. A large Jutish migration around the same time probably led to intermarriage between the Germanic tribes; certainly Cerdic's nephew Stuf was known as a Jute who became the first recognised king of the island. This Jutish kingdom ended with a bloody invasion by Caedwalla, King of Wessex, in 685, who slaughtered much of the population and forced surviving islanders to convert to Christianity, apparently in line with the whole of the rest of Britain.

Viking raids posed a problem towards the end of the Dark Ages, the island briefly serving as an important strategic base. But with the invasion of the Normans in 1066, and the construction of Carisbrooke Castle shortly after, the security of the island against further attack was greatly enhanced (and to this day there has not been any subsequent, fully successful invasion).

Formal governance created official ties with the mainland. William FitzOsbern – close relative of William the Conqueror – became the first Lord of the Isle of Wight, which became a hereditary title after Henry I granted it to FitzOsbern's nephew Richard de Redvers (the designer of Newport). The last Lord was Isabella de Fortibus, who was either persuaded or coerced into selling the island to King Edward I, and thus it was fully incorporated into the kingdom. Governors were appointed thereafter until the role was abolished in 1995.

Constant concern about a foreign invasion proved justified when in 1377 the French launched devastating raids on the ports of Newtown, Yarmouth and Newport – but they were forced to withdraw after failing to capture Carisbrooke Castle. This was 25 years after the Black Death had already decimated much of the population. After subsequent attacks, Yarmouth Castle was built by Henry VIII, but the island continued to generally decline until the 1600s, when a fledgling shipbuilding industry in Cowes proved successful and Newport began a gradual renaissance. The 1700s saw the rebuilding in grand style of the old manor houses at Gatcombe, Appuldurcombe and Swainston by their wealthy owners, perhaps reflecting relatively prosperous times for both the island and the country as a whole.

By the turn of the 1800s there was a new fashion for leisure travel among the well-to-do. In 1796 regular Solent crossings started between Portsmouth and Ryde, and several distinguished visitors came to discover what the island had to offer. The poet Tennyson relocated here for several years; and Dickens, Keats, Darwin and several other notables all visited. Two of today's premier attractions opened in this early period: the gorge of Shanklin Chine in 1817 and Blackgang Chine amusement park in 1843; and the multicoloured sands of

View towards Newport (Walk 18)

Alum Bay quickly became popular by word of mouth. Royalty were soon to get in on the act: King George IV was a member of the original Royal Yacht Club which founded Cowes Week in 1826, and his niece Queen Victoria fell in love with her 'dear, modest, unpretentious' Osborne House up the road in Whippingham. All this time smuggling was rife on the island, and it is said that the majority of the islanders were involved in some way with the rackets.

Railways arrived in the 1860s, and by 1900 there was an extremely comprehensive system in place, reaching Cowes, Freshwater and Ventnor – which had two stations. Tiny fishing hamlets reinvented themselves as important resorts, leading to a much greater influx of visitors. New seaside pleasure piers started to provide entertainment to the public, and soon the

island acquired a reputation for being a destination that all could enjoy. The island went from strength to strength in the early half of the 20th century, its infrastructure dramatically improving. During the Second World War the island was relatively unscathed, in part due to the old Palmerston Forts – such as the Needles Batteries – being restocked with contemporary weapons, so providing an effective defence. But Cowes suffered a major hit in 1942, and the war saw over 200 casualties in total.

Due to under-use, the railway system was a victim of government cuts under Dr Beeching and was all but dismantled by 1966, but tourism continued to thrive until the 1980s. The world's first hovercraft service started across the Solent in 1965, and in 1970 hundreds of thousands of music-lovers descended on East Afton Down

Alum Bay (Walk 4)

for the third Isle of Wight Festival to hear the likes of Jimi Hendrix and The Doors, severely straining infrastructure and causing locals and the council some alarm.

By the 1990s, however, a wealthier British population had discovered cheap foreign holidays, and the island developed a somewhat lower profile. Perhaps consequently, these days a large number of visitors are older people seeking peace and quiet, and traditional food and attractions. In recent times the island has not been exempt from economic problems, not helped by the decline in family tourism, but islanders remain happy and resolute.

MODERN SOCIETY

The 144,000 people of the Isle of Wight are a mixed bunch. In small villages such as Calbourne, Shorwell and Brighstone, the residents are typically older, comfortably off, and the epitome of Middle England. Whether 'overners' (the island word for outsiders) or 'caulkheads' (people born on the island), they are as proud of their village as they are of their island.

In the towns, where the majority of younger people live, the situation is a little more complex. At the time of writing, youth unemployment and a struggling economy have caused particular problems in Newport, Ryde and Sandown, and many of the brightest young people seek new opportunities on the mainland. A third type of resident is one who has a summer home here. Seaview, for example, is a village with a high proportion of second-homers.

As a county, the average age of the island's population is significantly higher than the national average, and

Thatched newsagent, Brighstone (Walks 12, 13 and 31)

this margin is increasing all the time, which is a real economic concern for the coming years (by 2026 36 per cent of the population is forecast to be over the current retirement age).

But despite these differences in the population, a small island almost by definition must have a sense of community, and there is a very strong one on the Isle of Wight. Serious crime is very rare; in fact, there is a distinct lack of 'edge' to the island, which perhaps reinforces the widely held notion that it is 'stuck in the 1950s'. The rather staid atmosphere today is presumably a great contrast with life before 'Victorianisation', when life in the fields was tough, smuggling was commonplace, and the forbidding coastline claimed numerous lives.

Arguably the main truly local event on the island's calendar is the annual Walking Festival fortnight in May, which culminates in 'Walk the Wight' day when thousands of people walk from Bembridge in the east to The Needles Landmark Attraction in the west for charity (shorter walks are also available). Walkers are given special permission to walk across some private land for the occasion. Much bigger events – such as the Isle of Wight Festival, its younger sibling Bestival, June's Round the Island yacht race, and August's Cowes Week – attract tens of thousands of visitors and keep the island in the spotlight.

Agriculture was the mainstay of the island's economy for centuries, but since Victorian times tourism has rivalled it. Although the era of the family fortnight holiday on the island is long dead, 'short-break' independent tourism is still at a respectable level and forecast to increase.

Highland cattle atop Shanklin Down (Walks 20 and 21)

PRINCIPAL LOCATIONS

Alum Bay (Walks 4, 5, 15) has been a major attraction for as long as tourists have been visiting the island on account of its magnificent and uniquely multicoloured cliffs, the colouring arising from the presence of various sulphates created by the oxidation of pyrite (ferrous sulphide). It is said that there are 21 colours – although presumably what constitutes a colour is open to definition – and sand from the cliffs has been a traditional purchase ever since the early 19th century. A seasonal chairlift that has been in operation since 1971 transports visitors from The Needles Landmark Attraction down some 60 metres to the bay.

Bembridge (Walks 9, 27, 30) is the most easterly settlement on the island and was until the 1870s a remote peninsula, as the sea extended as far southwest as Brading. In the medieval period it relied primarily on exporting stone, and the famous vessel the *Mary Rose* sank while trying to defend the village from a French invasion in 1545 (the French left after realising they didn't have enough resources to conquer the island). The isolated community built a church in the 1820s (rebuilt in the 1840s), but proper development got underway from 1878 when a road and rail embankment was built to link it to nearby St Helens. The village had a ferry service and a pier until the 1920s, when its heyday as a bustling tourist destination ended; the ferry was withdrawn, the pier demolished and the railway closed in 1953. Today's Bembridge is a rather sprawling village, but not unattractive. Look out for the rare 1929 K1 telephone kiosk in High Street.

There has been a settlement at **Brading** (Walks 26, 30, 32) since time immemorial, and until the 16th century it was a working port. After much of the harbour was successfully drained in 1878, the town somewhat lost its prosperity. Today, though, 'Ye Kynge's Towne of Bradynge' should be on every visitor's list, and three of the walks in this guide pass through it. Of interest are the 12th-century church, adjacent 18th-century Old Town Hall, the 13th-century Rectory Mansion (allegedly the oldest building on the island), the Lilliput Doll and Toy Museum, the bull ring (bull baiting was outlawed only in 1835) and Brading Roman Villa, one of the most important Roman sites in the UK.

The pretty cottages on the slender, twisting High Street are largely Victorian. Brading Day is celebrated on the first weekend of July to commemorate the granting of the town's first charter in 1285.

Brighstone (Walks 12, 13, 31) was called Brixton until the turn of the 20th century. It is a pretty enough place, and its Back of the Wight location is superb, sandwiched between dramatic downland and the sea. All three walks in this guide turn up North Street, which hosts an interesting little museum and equally quaint

Brighstone Forest from Cheverton Down (Walk 10)

post office. The village pub is proudly named after three local churchmen who ended their careers as bishops.

Brook (Walks 3, 4) is very much a blink-and-you've-missed-it hamlet with no identifiable core. Charles Seely purchased most of the village in 1859, including Brook House, a family residence until 1970, built on the site of an earlier manor house visited by King Henry VII. Italian general Garibaldi visited in 1864. In 1901 Seely built Brook Hill House for his son Frank on a nearby hill; the house was subsequently owned by the novelist and playwright JB Priestley. The church was largely rebuilt in the 1860s, having been severely fire damaged.

Evidence suggests that **Carisbrooke** (Walks 18, 19) was the principal settlement in Anglo-Saxon times. So it is no surprise that after the Conquest it was here that the Normans constructed their castle. An upstart new rival called Newport emerged late in the 12th century, its river-valley location helping it to flourish, and today Carisbrooke is considered a Newport suburb, despite the distinct village-like feel along its high street.

Cowes (or West Cowes) (Walk 7) is synonymous with all things nautical. It was here in August 1826 that the highly prestigious Royal Yacht Club, formed 11 years earlier with King George IV as a member, held its first yachting regatta, starting an annual tradition which continues to this day. Cowes is positively buzzing during Cowes Week, and the sheer number of events, boats and participants make it a very special time to visit. The Royal Yacht Squadron, as the club is now called, still calls Cowes its home (specifically Cowes Castle, originally a Tudor defence structure), and it is also the start and finish of the Round the Island race usually held every June. The town has medieval origins, but really came into its own in the 17th century, benefiting from passing trade and, later, shipbuilding (it is said that Cowes shipbuilders are the original 'caulkheads'). Stately residences such as Northwood House were built, while Cowes Week and the opening of the railway in 1862 (the first on the island) cemented the fortunes of the town. Today, even outside Cowes Week, the high street and esplanade feel hip and lively.

East Cowes (Walk 7, 8) is separated from Cowes by the River Medina, but is quite literally linked to it by a chain ferry, and the town mimicked Cowes' fortunes from the 17th century. Notable buildings include Norris Castle and the all-but-demolished East Cowes Castle – home of architect John Nash, who designed the town's church and is buried in its churchyard. East Cowes continued to specialise in shipbuilding when its more glitzy neighbour turned to sailing. 'High society' and kudos came to East Cowes in a big way, however, when Victoria and Albert purchased and greatly extended Osborne House in the 1840s. The town centre is low key, but if you have an hour to spare it is pleasant to walk along the esplanade to the grounds of Norris Castle.

More a district than a village, **Freshwater** (Walks 4, 5, 14, 15, 19) is the largest urban settlement west of Cowes and Newport. It is made

Cowes Marina (Walk 7)

up of several hamlets, such as the old village itself, School Green, Norton Green, Middleton and Locksley; although the coastal resorts of Norton, Colwell, Totland and Freshwater Bay – and, in fact, the whole peninsula to the west of the Western Yar (technically an island in itself) – can also be included in a loose definition. Only disparate communities existed before the 19th century – the parish neatly consisted of Norton, Weston, Easton, Sutton (today's Freshwater Bay) and Middleton – and, as with the east-coast resorts, development was accelerated with the coming of the railway in 1889. Rather than an urban sprawl, however, there exist several charming pockets of countryside between the residential areas: Walk 15 gives a good introduction. Distinguished

17th-century scientist Robert Hooke was born here, but it is as the home of Alfred Lord Tennyson for several years that Freshwater is famed; his Farringford House still stands, and there is a striking monument to him on top of Tennyson Down.

Pronounced 'godzill' by locals, the village of **Godshill** (Walks 23, 31, 33) is one of the principal inland excursion destinations and so can become very crowded in summer. Nevertheless, a pretty place is a pretty place, and the tourists who visit are not likely to spoil one's enjoyment. The village consists of an attractive main street with numerous thatched buildings and a disproportionate number of tearooms. A visit to the model village (open since 1952) is well worthwhile, as is the ascent

Shop, Freshwater Bay (Walk 15)

Prince Consort Building in Ryde (Walk 8)

to the 14th-century church and the lovely thatched cottages close by. The church is remarkable for its 15th-century 'Lily Cross' painting, and is the second church on the site. The first was built shortly before the Norman Conquest; as the church was being built, its foundations 'miraculously' made their way from a different spot to the current hilltop location. This was taken as a sign from God, hence the name Godshill.

The island's capital, **Newport** (Walks 17, 18, 29, 30), is a small, relaxed place, but large enough to accommodate a high street featuring both chain and independent shops, and is worth a half-day's visit. The Minster on St Thomas' Square is Victorian, having replaced a 12th-century church. Notable streets are Quay Street and Watchbell Lane, both explored on Walk 29. The town was founded around 1180 by Richard de Redvers, then Lord of the Island, as a port settlement near Carisbrooke, and it was he who introduced the grid system of streets that still exists today. Its heyday was in Georgian times, following the decline in fortune of nearby Newtown and prior to the growth of Ryde and Cowes.

Known as the Gateway to the Island, **Ryde** (Walks 8, 9, 26) is something of an enigma. The town does not exude sophistication and has clearly seen better days, but its idiosyncrasies are beguiling, and it actually possesses a wealth of fine early 19th-century architecture which goes largely unnoticed. Union Street, the steep commercial avenue ascending from the esplanade, was built in 1780 to link the villages of Lower and Upper Ryde. This helped form one town, which really came into its own in Victorian times as the first stop for the thousands of people who came to the island for their holidays (the Portsmouth ferry started in 1825). The pier dates from 1814 and the ornate iron balustrades were installed around 1880.

Sandown (Walks 1, 9) is the most northerly of the three major resorts on the east coast, set in the centre of 6-mile Sandown Bay behind a long sandy beach. As with Shanklin and Ventnor, the town started to thrive with the coming of the railway, and for about a century was the

quintessential island resort for families wanting a bit of no-frills sun and fun. Since the decline of family tourism, however, the town has a slightly rundown feel even in summer, not having the charm of Shanklin or the magnificent location of Ventnor to sustain it. That said, it does boast the only surviving pleasure pier on the island, the bay's seascape from Culver Cliff to the southeast downs is enviable, and the town still makes a perfectly good, practical base for a walking holiday.

Despite being just 2 miles from Ryde, there is a distinctness and certain integrity about **Seaview** (Walks 9, 27), and it certainly feels a 'cut above' its westerly neighbour. Fine old houses abound, many of which today are seasonal second homes, and its residents include a large number

Sandown Bay (Walk 9)

of retirees. Development started in the early 1800s, and its crowning glory was a marvellous pier built in 1881 – one of only two in the country designed as a series of suspension bridges – but it was destroyed in a storm on Boxing Day 1950, a devastating event for village and island alike. Although Seaview is technically a resort, its charm lies in its upmarket status, so unlike its larger neighbours further south it does not court the masses.

Along with Sandown to the north and Ventnor to the south, **Shanklin** (Walks 1, 20, 21, 22, 23, 31) is one of the principal bases for visitors, offering an abundance of accommodation. It is indeed an ideal place to stay, with clean beaches, several independent shops, the quaint if rather vacuous Old Village, and a generally pleasant atmosphere. Like Sandown, transport links are frequent to both Ryde and Newport. The resort, including the Old Village, only really developed during the 19th century courtesy of the railway, and visitors – including Darwin, Dickens, Austen and Keats – flocked to rest on the beach, visit the dramatic Chine, taste the allegedly health-restoring spring water and (from 1890) visit the pier, sadly destroyed in the hurricane of 1987.

Shorwell (Walks 10, 11, 32) and Brighstone are the principal villages on the Back of the Wight. While the latter is larger and closer to the coastline, the former has a humbler, more sheltered and introspective feel. Certainly it is photogenic, with thatched stone cottages and a charming medieval church (originally 12th century but almost rebuilt in the 15th). Less well known are Shorwell's secluded three manor houses, all dating from Tudor (West Court, Wolverton Manor) to early Stuart times (North Court). The village was extended somewhat in the 1980s, but its historic core has been left unmolested.

Surely to most eyes the classiest and most attractive of the island's three major seaside resorts, **Ventnor** (Walks 1, 2, 20, 26, 33) was little more than a fishing hamlet before the 19th century, centred around a mill and waterfall to the east of the modern town's promenade (the mill is long gone but the waterfall – now known as The Cascade – remains). The turning point came in 1829 when renowned physician Sir James Clark extolled the virtues of the area's sunny and mild microclimate and well-heeled mainlanders took notice. The 1840s especially saw great expansion and the building of three successive piers, the third being demolished in 1993 after fire damage. Another major boost came with the arrival of the railway from Ryde in 1866, and to a lesser extent a branch line from Merstone in 1900. Churchill, Gandhi, Marx and Elgar are just some of the notables to have travelled here, and contemporary visitors often include the island's botanic gardens in their itineraries.

Yarmouth (Walks 5, 6, 13, 14) is one of the oldest towns on the island (reputedly also the smallest in the UK) and has quite a special ambience: graceful and immediately appealing. The town's origins go back to Saxon times, and it was mentioned in the *Domesday Book* as *Ermud* ('muddy estuary'), but the turning point came in 1135 when it received its charter. Trade increased, and King John made the town his personal headquarters twice in the early 13th century. Yarmouth managed to withstand 14th-century French raids (unlike nearby Newtown) but, as a precaution, 200 years later Yarmouth Castle was built by King Henry VIII, and can be visited today (www.english-heritage.org.uk). Yarmouth is the destination port for ferries from Lymington and is the perfect starting point for some easy walking along the Coastal Path and beside the Western Yar.

TOP TEN ATTRACTIONS

If or when you fancy a break from walking, or the weather demands it, there are a number of recommended places to visit:

- **Osborne House** Queen Victoria and Prince Albert's holiday home is the most significant attraction on the island (www.english-heritage.org.uk).
- **Carisbrooke Castle** (www.english-heritage.org.uk). See Walk 18.
- **Brading Roman Villa** (www.bradingromanvilla.org.uk). There is also a lesser-known Roman villa in Newport.
- **Isle of Wight Steam Railway** (www.iwsteamrailway.co.uk). The steam railway can be used to get to the start of Walk 25.
- **Dinosaur Isle**, Sandown (www.dinosaurisle.com).
- **Museum of Island History** (search www.iwight.com). Small, under-visited museum in Newport's Guildhall. See Walk 29.
- **Dimbola Lodge** (www.dimbola.co.uk). The Freshwater home of Victorian photographer Julia Margaret Cameron, often hosting some fine exhibitions. See Walk 15.
- **Blackgang Chine amusement park** (www.blackgangchine.com). First opened its doors in 1843. Definitely more for young children, but also fun if you're young at heart. See Walk 2.
- **Robin Hill Country Park** (www.robin-hill.com). Blackgang's younger sibling (both were started by the Dabell family).
- **Needles Landmark Attraction** (www.theneedles.co.uk). Take the famous chairlift down to Alum Bay.

There is a host of other smaller attractions too, so check out the relevant literature in print or online (see Appendix B).

WILDLIFE

*Wildflowers near Bonchurch
(Walks 1 and 21)*

The wide variety of plants and eco-systems found on the island can be attributed not only to its diverse range of landscape – including woodland, downs, wide estuaries, tidal creeks, marshland and large protected nature reserves, such as Brading Marshes – but also to a year-round temperate climate.

Especially in the northeast, the island is filled with rich mixed woodland, much of it ancient. Previous policies of coniferous planting which, it was assumed, would assist the red squirrel population are now being overturned, and the trend is now for more planting of native (deciduous) species. Plants unique (or almost) to the island include Martin's ramping-fumitory, early gentian, field cow-wheat, and the exceptionally rare wood calamint. There are also 27 distinct species of orchid that can be found here.

In terms of animal life, the island is special not just for its renowned red squirrel population, but also for dormice, which are common in much of the island's woodland. It is also a great place to see birds, with notable numbers of wintering species such as Brent geese, teal and widgeon, which complement other species commonly seen on the island such as the magnificent peregrine falcon, nightjars, woodcocks, long-eared owls, firecrests, cormorants, shags and, of course, gulls. Newtown Harbour is a particularly special place for birdwatching; a bird hide has been built for that purpose, where sightings are

Jetty, Newtown Harbour (Walk 6)

recorded. The island is one of the few places left in the country where the beautiful wasp-coloured Granville fritillary butterfly can be seen hovering around the sea cliffs.

The island also has a number of wildlife-related tourist attractions such as the Monkey Haven, Amazon World and Butterfly World, as well as the larger Isle of Wight Zoo based in Sandown and Ventnor Botanic Garden. The garden has introduced wall lizards, the largest UK colony of which exists in the wild between it and the town centre.

WHEN TO GO

The wonderful thing about the Isle of Wight is that the climate is conducive to walking at any time of year. Winters are generally milder than in most places in the UK and snow is a rare event, even on higher ground. Conversely, summer temperatures tend to be lower than most of the south of England, with a refreshing breeze, so there are not many days when it is too hot to walk. Rainfall is about average for southern England – so unlikely to be a significant issue. And last but not least, the island is a suntrap: Shanklin is widely regarded as one of the sunniest places in the UK, and neighbouring Ventnor has its own warm and sunny microclimate.

As well as the benefits of lower accommodation prices and fewer tourists, winter can be a great time

Cowes to Southampton catamaran (Walk 7)

Frosty scene in Steyne Wood (Walk 27)

to walk by the sea, and a week spent walking the Coastal Path in the colder months is recommended, especially for hardier walkers as one or two sections can be plagued by boggy ground. There are usually numerous pubs to warm you up, and buses generally run to the same timetable year-round. For bad-weather days, many of the larger attractions remain open throughout the year.

The season really gets going from early April; tourist numbers and accommodation prices increase, although even in the height of summer the island seldom feels crowded and the pace stays relaxed. May brings beautiful fields of fragrant rapeseed and wildflowers, and summer and autumn are perfect for

exploring the island's scattered forests and woodland. From the end of October, when the trees are shedding their leaves and visitors start to leave, walkers in the know continue to explore and appreciate the island.

GETTING TO THE ISLAND

The idea of a bridge across the Solent is periodically mooted locally, as the mainland is just a few miles away, but many islanders are opposed to this idea for practical, ideological and aesthetic reasons.

Therefore, as has been the case for thousands of years, the only way to get to the island is by sea. The following **car-ferry services** can also be used by foot passengers.

Mainland	Island	Journey time	Operator
Portsmouth Harbour	Fishbourne (near Ryde)	40min	Wightlink
Southampton Town Quay	East Cowes	1hr	Red Funnel
Lymington Pier	Yarmouth	35min	Wightlink

The following services are for **foot passengers** only.

Mainland	Island	Journey time	Seacraft	Operator
Portsmouth Harbour Station	Ryde Pier	20min	Catamaran	Wightlink
Southsea (Clarence Pier)	Ryde Esplanade	10min	Hovercraft	Hovertravel
Southampton Town Quay	(West) Cowes	25min	Catamaran	Red Funnel

The above services vary in frequency from every 15min to every 90min; timetables can be easily accessed online. Tickets for car and foot passengers can be bought both in advance and at the port, and there are frequently special offers available, so look at the operators' websites before purchasing (see Appendix B).

Through train/ferry tickets can be bought to any station on the Island Line (i.e. between Ryde Pier and Shanklin), and to Cowes, East Cowes and Yarmouth.

GETTING AROUND

The island's road network is good, yet traffic is noticeably light, and driving along the many rural roads and country lanes can be delightful. Parking is often free or low cost, and details are provided for each walk.

Taking a car onto the ferry can be expensive, however, so you may wish to consider leaving it on the mainland. The island's bus service, operated by Southern Vectis, is excellent: comprehensive, fast and usually extremely reliable. All the walks in this book are accessible by bus, and a journey across the island from Ryde or Sandown to Alum Bay takes about 90min. Before heading out on a walk make sure that you obtain one of Southern Vectis' user-friendly bus timetables, available at Newport, Yarmouth and Ryde bus stations and from the Southern Vectis website (www.islandbuses.info). They show all the bus routes on the island and are an essential navigation aid (the website also provides a detailed

network map). In summary the main routes are as follows.

'Needles Breezer' bus at the Old Battery (Walk 4)

Route	Recommended use between	Current daily frequency
1	Newport–Cowes	Usually 6–8 per hour
2	Newport–Shanklin/Sandown	2 per hour
	Ryde–Shanklin/Godshill	2 per hour
3	Newport–Ventnor	2 per hour
	Ryde–Ventnor	2 per hour
4	Ryde–East Cowes	1 per hour
5	Newport–East Cowes	3 per hour Mon–Sat; 2 per hour Sundays
6	Newport–Niton	1 per hour Mon–Sat; 4 journeys Sundays
	Ventnor–Niton/Chale	1 per hour Mon–Sat; 4 journeys Sundays
7	Newport–Alum Bay	2 per hour (route varies between Carisbrooke and Yarmouth)
8	Newport–Sandown	1 per hour
	Ryde–Bembridge	1 per hour
9	Newport–Ryde	6 per hour Mon–Sat; 4 per hour Sundays
12	Newport–Freshwater Bay	4–5 journeys per day

Single and return tickets can be bought on any bus to any destination on the island, even if you need to change buses, but daily or longer bus passes provide best value.

During the tourist season there are additional open-top buses, and a trip on at least one of these is highly recommended. These trips are currently included in the price of bus passes, and as they are hop-on-hop-off services they can be used as conventional buses. The routes currently in operation are the Needles Breezer (a circuit from Yarmouth via Freshwater Bay and the Needles) and the Downs Breezer (a circuit from Ryde taking in Robin Hill Adventure Park, Amazon World and Ashey Down).

There is also a seasonal Island Coaster service running clockwise from Ryde to Yarmouth every morning and returning from Alum Bay every afternoon (up to three services daily). This can be especially handy for travelling between one of the eastern resorts and the Back of the Wight. Again, bus passes are currently valid on this service.

A useful train service (officially called the Island Line) runs between Ryde Pier and Shanklin, a relic of the many steam railway lines which once criss-crossed the island. A quirk is that the trains are 1930s London Underground stock, which is often a source of amusement for visitors stepping off the catamaran in Ryde. Trains are generally every 30min, timed to connect with the catamaran.

ACCOMMODATION

Most visitors stay in one of the seaside resorts on the east of the island, Sandown, Shanklin or Ventnor, where

Cottage in St Lawrence (walk 2)

there are hotels and B&Bs for all budgets. Sandown generally offers the lowest rates and Ventnor the highest, with prices varying according to season but 'mini-peaking' over Christmas and New Year. Websites like Tripadvisor (www.tripadvisor.co.uk) are handy to find the most popular places, but there are no significant concerns over standards.

While the resorts certainly make excellent choices for a walking break, there are less conventional alternatives. Interesting and often upmarket places can be found in areas such as Seaview and Niton Undercliff; and cottages, camping and other self-catering options can be found all over the island, sometimes in pleasingly remote locations. Newport has budget chain hotels and a few boutique hotels, and makes a good base for travellers relying on public transport who wish to visit the whole island and prefer the bustle of a town to staying by the sea. Ryde and Cowes also offer a sprinkling of accommodation.

For those on a strict budget, there are YHA hostels in Totland (open throughout the year) and Brighstone (summer holiday only).

WHAT TO TAKE

What to take on a walk depends largely on your disposition, but every walker should always take the following essentials.

- **Weather-appropriate clothing**. Remember to check the forecast for the whole day and be prepared for all reasonable eventualities. More breathable fabrics will aid your comfort.
- **Lightweight walking boots** will be needed for most walks even on dry days, so should be regarded as essential. After rain, boots are essential on every walk.
- **Food and water** in inverse proportion to availability of refreshment retailers (and more than you think you need)
- **Sun cream**, **sunglasses** and a **sun-hat** when necessary
- Basic **first-aid kit**

For longer walks or in more remote areas, it may be prudent to bring a mobile phone, GPS device, compass and emergency torch and/or whistle, especially if walking alone. The 1:25,000 Ordnance Survey map for the Isle of Wight (Explorer sheet OL29) – larger scale than the map used for this book – would also be a good investment, and a pedometer would assist in following directions. Finally, knowledge of tide times may assist with some walks (see website listed in Appendix B).

SAFETY

A great advantage of walking on the island is that it is possible to enjoy magnificent scenery without seriously losing your way, and the chances of encountering any nasty accidents are slim. But if a problem were to occur, habitation would never be far away, and there is an A&E department at St Mary's Hospital in Newport.

Keep an eye on the weather as high winds – which can occur frequently – can cause difficulties both on the downs and along the coast. An entirely windless day, sunny or cloudy, often makes walking on the island idyllic, but the obvious tip on windy days is to choose a walk following the wind's direction. And if the forecast looks dubious choose a walk where it is possible to finish early. Finally, don't walk on the downs when mist or fog is forecast, and treat clifftops with respect.

Stinging nettles and insects can be a minor nuisance in the warmer months, but the island is not significantly affected by ticks, which are becoming more common in the UK and can carry Lyme disease. You may wish to take precautions, however. Curious cows may also be about on some of the walks, which can be a bit unnerving at first, but just ignore them and they'll lose interest.

Lastly, take care not to over-exert yourself, especially on remote walks that can't easily be shortened.

THE COUNTRYSIDE

The island is a beautiful place, so do try to keep it that way. The fundamental principle is to leave no trace of your visit except your goodwill to the people you meet.

You should use common sense if straying off footpaths, even though the CROW Act (2000) provides the walker with the freedom to walk off-path in certain areas, such as downland and coastal areas, irrespective

Always treat clifftops with respect (Walk 2)

of whether they are privately owned. Such open access areas are often indicated by signs showing a brown, circular symbol with a person walking, and are also marked on Ordnance Survey Explorer maps.

WALKING IN GROUPS

If you are walking with even just one other person, remember that walking speeds and abilities vary, and that the sensible (and polite) thing to do is to choose a walk which can be accomplished by the least able person in the group and pace it to the slowest.

WALKING WITH CHILDREN

The island is well known as a family destination, and some of the walks in this book would be suitable for children. Indulging in a few walks could definitely enhance a family holiday, and the introductory information for each walk will help parents decide which might be appropriate. Two very easy hikes for all the family to enjoy are the Coastal Path stretches from Sandown to Shanklin and from Ryde to Seaview – passing the playground at Puckpool Park (Walks 1 and 9 respectively). Particular care should, of course, be taken near cliff edges.

USING THIS GUIDE

The 33 walks in this book could keep the walker occupied for weeks. Each route offers a unique experience, and is worth doing both for its own sake and to add to one's appreciation of the island's diversity. This emphasis on quality has meant that many

Bird hide, Newtown Harbour Nature Reserve (Walk 16)

of the council's official trails are not included because, curiously, they don't quite cut the mustard. The route summary table in Appendix A shows the walks included.

The walks begin with the Coastal Path (Walks 1–9), followed by walks in West Wight (Walks 10–19) and East Wight (Walks 20–33). Ranging from 7.4km (4.6 miles) to 29.3km (18.3 miles), the routes explore not only popular areas such as around the Needles and along the Coastal Path, but also parts of the island which are less well known to visitors, such as Parkhurst Forest, Ashey and Mersley Downs, and the Niton Undercliff. Except in the height of summer you should encounter few other walkers, especially on the lesser-known paths, and indeed one of the advantages of walking here is the peace and quiet that it brings.

Footpaths are generally in very good order across the island, although mud can be a problem at any time of year, and significantly so outside summer. Waymarking is generally good; all official footpaths and bridleways have a unique reference based on the parish in which they are located – so, for example, footpath F14 is located in Freshwater – and these are almost always included on signposts. The council's official trails, such as the Coastal Path and Tennyson Trail, are named on signposts only sporadically, and following the trails using these signposts alone would be difficult.

All walks are accessible by public transport: to the start, from the finish, and often from at least somewhere in between. All abilities are catered for, with some of the easier walks being appropriate for older people and children (see 'Walking with children'). At the other end of the scale, the interconnectedness of many walks may lead hardy walkers to do two or three in one day.

Information is provided at the start of every walk description about its distance, difficulty grade, required walking time, refreshment facilities, access to the start and from the finish by public transport, where to park and opportunities to finish early. Walking time estimates are for fit, regular walkers and do not include rest stops. Add at least 25 per cent to the times given if you are not a confident walker and/or wish to allow time for breaks (which is much advised). 'Grade' refers mainly to the level of fitness needed to complete the walk, irrespective of length. So a long but mainly flat walk would be graded 'easy', whereas a short and very hilly walk would be graded 'moderate'. To a lesser extent, factors such as ease of route-finding and condition of the terrain have also been taken into consideration.

Ordnance Survey mapping is included for each walk with the route clearly marked. In the route description, key places along the route that also appear on the map extract are shown in **bold** to help with navigation.

COASTAL PATH

The Needles (Walk 4)

INTRODUCTION

Walk number	Walk title	Distance	Time
1	Sandown to Ventnor	10.5km (6.6 miles)	2½hr
2	Ventnor to Chale	12.3km (7.7 miles)	3½hr
3	Chale to Brook	13.2km (8.3 miles)	3hr
4	Brook to Alum Bay	11.9km (7.4 miles)	3hr
5	Alum Bay to Yarmouth	8.7km (5.4 miles)	2½hr
6	Yarmouth to Shalfleet	12.7km (7.9 miles)	3hr
7	Shalfleet to East Cowes	16.7km (10.4 miles)	4hr
8	East Cowes to Ryde	12.7km (7.9 miles)	3hr
9	Ryde to Sandown	19.1km (11.9 miles)	5½hr

If recreational walking is the island's crown, then the Coastal Path of about 70 miles must be its jewel. The path circumnavigates the island, and throughout its length offers ever-changing scenic variety. Compare for instance the wildness of the Back of the Wight to the very tame stretch between Sandown and Shanklin, or the sheer drama of the far south and far west sections with the gentle inland meanderings between Cowes and Yarmouth. Every stage of the Coastal Path is worth doing in order to appreciate the sheer diversity of the island's coastline.

The Path is presented here as nine stages in a clockwise direction. While the route can of course be walked on consecutive days, accommodation is very limited west of Cowes

and Ventnor, and the coastline is no exception, so it may be prudent to make good use of the fast and usually frequent bus services for these stages to get between your accommodation and the start or finish of the route. Only the southwest stages served by infrequent bus route 12 could cause logistical difficulties in this regard. Due to the ever-present problems of erosion and landslips, there may be diversions in place on some short stretches, but conversely paths closed for some time in Bembridge and Colwell because of landslips have recently been professionally and sensitively restored.

Finally, it is intended that the Isle of Wight Coastal Path be included as part of the England Coast Path set to be completed in 2020.

SOUTH COAST

WALK 1

Sandown to Ventnor

Start	Sandown Pier
Finish	Ventnor
Distance	10.5km (6.6 miles)
Grade	Easy to Shanklin, then moderate
Time	2½hr
Refreshments	A sprinkling of seasonal cafés between Sandown and Shanklin. One seasonal café beyond Shanklin (9.7km).
Public transport	To start: bus routes 2, 3 and 8, and train (short walk); from finish: bus routes 3 and 6
Parking	Long-stay car park in Station Avenue; also possible beside the pier
Early finish	Lake Station (1.2km), Shanklin Old Village (4.7km, bus route 3), top of Devil's Chimney (7.4km, bus route 3)

The heavily used clifftop path between the two premier resorts on the island, Sandown and Shanklin, makes for an easy, brisk 45min stroll and can even be enjoyed at night. After descending to the beach past the entrance to Shanklin Chine, the route climbs the numerous Appley Steps to lovely Rylstone Gardens in the Old Village and continues up Luccombe Road with its fine, dignified houses. The Landslip follows – a riot of greenery with intermittent sea views. Make a short detour to the old church at Bonchurch, and end this particularly varied walk along the sea wall linking Bonchurch and Ventnor.

Facing the pier at **Sandown** (accommodation, supermarkets, pubs, cafés, restaurants, shops, toilets) turn right. After 200 metres go right by the Ferncliff Path sign to head steeply uphill. Shortly go left up steps and left at the top through Ferncliff Gardens to emerge on a clifftop

It is also possible to walk to Shanklin along the shore but the clifftop path is arguably more satisfying.

map continues on page 42

path. ◀ This easy concrete path may be rather tame, but that in no way detracts from the enjoyment: the sea views are mostly uninterrupted, and there are frequent benches on which to sit and enjoy the view.

By a café in **Lake** (accommodation, supermarket, pubs, restaurants, shops) in 750 metres, it is possible to shorten the walk by turning right on footpath SS62, which leads in a few minutes to the station. A minor Coastal Path diversion may still be in operation 650 metres beyond: you are led onto a road where you turn left, then after just 60 metres turn left again to rejoin the clifftop path, now at the start of **Shanklin** (accommodation, supermarkets, pubs, cafés, restaurants, shops, toilets). Pass the seasonal lift (built 1891) in a further 1.2km and continue on the undulating path, soon passing the back gardens of some

Keats Green

rather quaint-looking hotels in Keats Green, named after the poet, who frequently visited Shanklin. At the end of the green, descend past a metal barrier all the way to the shore, perhaps visiting **Shanklin Chine** halfway down – it's worth paying the admission charge if only to experience the island's oldest tourist attraction.

> **Shanklin Chine** was opened to the public as early as 1817, and was as popular in the Victorian era as it is now. As well as its beautiful foliage, pretty trails and diverse bird- and animal-life – including resident chipmunks – the Chine boasts a 12m (40ft) waterfall and romantic summer-night illuminations. There is also a permanent exhibition about the wartime Pipe Line Under The Ocean (PLUTO), which ran from the Chine to Cherbourg transporting petrol for Allied troops. The idea came from Lord Mountbatten and was apparently very successful – the enemy never knew about it, and 56,000 gallons of petrol per day was transported this way during 1944.

41

Turn sharp right at the bottom of the slope to walk along the shore; pass the Fisherman's Cottage, then after 150 metres go sharp right up the inconspicuous 'Appley Steps'. At the top, although the Coastal Path continues straight ahead, detour through pretty Rylstone Gardens first. Continue with the sea to the right this time; then when the path ends, return through the gardens, pausing to admire the charming small hotel in its grounds and perhaps have a cuppa in the tea rooms.

Aim for, and exit at, the far right corner of the gardens. Turn right then immediately left to ascend Luccombe Road with its large elegant houses. ◄ In 400 metres turn right on a signposted footpath into a field, and immediately left, keeping close to the hedge (or stay on the road if too muddy). Go over a stile in the far corner to return to and continue along the road, enjoying lovely sea views.

Keep straight ahead at a junction and shortly continue on a footpath through woodland. Ignore ways off. After 1.3km, head up steps to enter **The Landslip** (so called because of the erosion and intermittent landslides that have affected the area since the last ice age), again ignoring ways off the main path and following Coastal Path signs.

After 550 metres, to shorten the walk, take V65c up the notorious 'Devil's Chimney': a tough 10min climb up 225 steps, one section narrowly wedged between cliffs. ◄

Otherwise, the path continues to wind around The Landslip's foliage. After 800 metres, turn right – initially up three steps. After 150 metres bear left and left again at

To end the walk, or perhaps have lunch, turn sharp right on exiting the gardens to reach the centre of Shanklin Old Village (pubs, cafés, restaurants, shops, toilets) via the upper gate of the Chine. Bus stops are just up the hill.

At the road behind the Smugglers Haven turn right for bus stops.

Sea wall to Ventnor

the next junction, but not before detouring a short way to the right to see isolated St Boniface Church at **Bonchurch** (limited accommodation, pub, restaurant), nestled in its pretty churchyard (see Walk 21).

Shortly after this junction there is a choice of paths; take either, as both eventually emerge on a sea wall at Wheelers Bay (if taking the upper path bear left at the end). Continue along it to reach the seafront at **Ventnor** (accommodation, supermarkets, pubs, cafés, restaurants, shops, toilets). For the main shopping street and bus stop, turn sharp right up the slope opposite the Hygeia mosaic at the start of the seafront proper, and continue up Pier Street to the T-junction. Take a peak into Alexandra Gardens on the way: Elgar honeymooned at number three.

WALK 2
Ventnor to Chale

Start	Ventnor seafront
Finish	Chale
Distance	12.3km (7.7 miles)
Grade	Moderate
Time	3½hr
Refreshments	Steephill Cove (1.7km), Ventnor Botanic Garden (2.3km), St Lawrence (4.9km), Niton (8.3km) (off route)
Public transport	To start: bus routes 3 and 6; from finish: bus route 6
Parking	Eastern Esplanade or La Falaise long-stay car parks
Early finish	Beyond Niton (8.3km) the route is never far from the road (bus route 6).

This must count among the best walks on the island, so pick a sunny day to appreciate it fully. After ascending the cliffs west of Ventnor and passing the botanic gardens, the walk reaches the classy village of St Lawrence, a peaceful and – so it would seem – eminently desirable place to live. Ascend onto even higher cliffs and soon there are magnificent views towards St Catherine's Lighthouse and a quite special sense of serenity. But the best is yet to come as Windy Corner is approached and the entire southwest coast (Back of the Wight) is spread out before you, all the way to the iconic white cliffs of High Down. The route descends first to the country's oldest amusement park at Blackgang Chine and, finally, to Chale.

Walk west along the esplanade at **Ventnor** (accommodation, supermarkets, pubs, cafés, restaurants, shops, toilets) and continue uphill. Walk through La Falaise car park and continue on the cliff path beyond. ◀

Stay on the paths nearest the sea (although one or two may shortly arrive at a dead end), eventually reaching Steephill Cove (restaurants/cafés, toilets) – a lovely low-key place to rest and perhaps swim. Ascend the slope at the far end of the cove, turning sharp left after

Lizards were introduced to Ventnor in the early 19th century and a colony has developed on the cliffs around this car park, so keep a look out.

60 metres, ascending steps and turning left again. The path soon borders the seaward side of **Ventnor Botanic Garden**. You may wish to take time to explore the garden, which also has a café with outdoor seating. Entry is via a gate on the right (admission fee payable).

> **Ventnor Botanic Garden** is protected from northerly winds by its Undercliff setting, and its warm and sunny microclimate has enabled unusual exotic and subtropical species to thrive here, including cacti. There is a Mediterranean garden, complete with an olive grove and lizards; a palm garden featuring the oldest palms in Britain; and Australian, New Zealand, Oriental and South African gardens among others. There is also an interesting display about the days when the garden was part of the Royal National Hospital for Diseases of the Chest, founded in 1868.

Beyond the gardens, you are less likely to encounter fellow walkers. After coming out into the open, the path stays on top of the sea cliffs for about another 1.6km, then turns inland, now in **St Lawrence** (village shop). In 150 metres turn left through a gate; then where the main path swings left, branch right, ignoring path offshoots, and turn left at the lane above. Turn right at the T-junction and

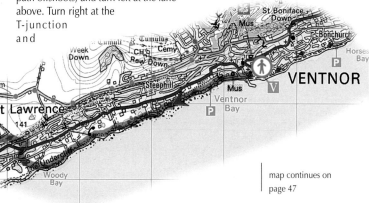

map continues on page 47

45

View over St Lawrence

walk up to the main road, permanently closed to through traffic due to a landslip. Continue up Spindlers Road, past the turn for the village shop. At Seven Sisters Road turn left. ◀ In 80 metres take footpath V81 which ascends steeply to 'High Hat', towering over St Lawrence.

Alternatively, go right for a pleasant 20min-return detour to the old church and peace gardens; descend right at The Shute.

Continue west along the cliff path, ignoring ways off. Then after 2.6km (shortly after the path turns inland), ignore a track coming in from the left and turn left at the T-junction shortly afterwards to reach a road on the outskirts of **Niton** (shops, toilets). ◀ Turn right and immediately sharp left up a driveway. After about 800 metres there is an incredible view towards **St Catherine's Point** – the island's southern tip – and its tenant lighthouse.

Turn right here for the village centre and left for bus stops.

Pass a signpost and bench a little further on. To descend to the lighthouse from here see Walk 24, but otherwise continue – now on the west of the island and about to start your exploration of the southwest coast. The

46

iconic chalk cliffs of High Down soon come into view, and eventually – just short of what is known as Windy Corner – there is the first view of the entire southwest coastline (Back of the Wight).

The path shortly swings inland – the view now encompassing St Catherine's Oratory Lighthouse

Looking towards St Catherine's Lighthouse

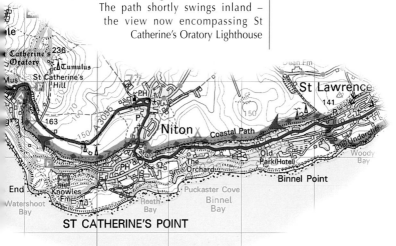

47

on the hill above (see Walk 11) and Blackgang Chine below (ignore a steeply descending path towards it) – and emerges at a car park. Near the road turn left through a wooden gate on a descending path. In 250 metres maintain your current direction along the right edge of a field. Turn right over a stile after 100 metres and continue along the roadside verge, bearing right at the **Blackgang** roundabout (or left for the short detour to **Blackgang Chine**).

Since 1843 **Blackgang Chine** has been the site of one of the island's main attractions, despite the chine itself no longer existing due to frequent landslips. It's an understated but surprisingly enjoyable, old-fashioned amusement park enhanced by its clifftop garden setting. One of its first exhibits, still on show today, was a whale skeleton found on the shore. During a visit by Queen Mary, her hat was knocked off her head by one of the skeleton's bones, and immediately afterwards the offending bone was removed from the skeleton! Remarkably the park is still owned by the family who built it (the Dabells), although it has been a frequent victim of erosion, notably in 1994 when a sizeable chunk was destroyed.

In 400 metres turn left onto a signposted footpath, then right at a T-junction. Back at the road turn left and immediately right past the church to the bus stops at **Chale** (limited accommodation, pub).

Chale Church retains few of its 12th-century origins, having been largely reconstructed in the 15th century, when the tower was added. The village is associated with tales of smugglers and shipwrecks, and the churchyard is full of unfortunates who perished at sea.

WALK 3

Chale to Brook

Start	Chale Church
Finish	Brook Chine, Brook
Distance	13.2km (8.3 miles)
Grade	Easy apart from short steep descents and ascents at Shepherd's and Grange chines
Time	3hr
Refreshments	Café at Isle of Wight Pearl (10.2km)
Public transport	To start: bus route 6; from finish: bus route 12 (limited service)
Parking	Car park about 200 metres north of the church
Early finish	Near Brighstone (8.4km) or anywhere along the coastal road for the afternoon seasonal Island Coaster bus service

The Back of the Wight's heavily eroded coastline is bleak, wild and ruggedly beautiful. Dubbed 'The Ships' Graveyard', it has claimed countless vessels and lives over the centuries, with many of the victims ending up in Chale churchyard. Contrast this stretch of the Coastal Path with that from Cowes to Gurnard; both offer very different ways of experiencing the island's coastline. In the right conditions this should be an easy, serene walk with lovely views, perfect for contemplation or conversation. But pick a calm day: in rain or even just brisk northerly or westerly winds the outing can turn into a slog, especially as there is little shelter and few public transport options en route.

Chale (limited accommodation, pub) is a small, indistinct village, so those coming by bus need to be eagle-eyed or ask the driver for Chale Church. At the T-junction by the church, head west towards the sea.

This is **Military Road**, constructed in the 1930s to replace a 19th-century defence track. It follows

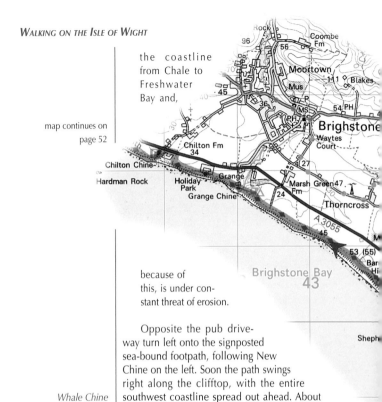

the coastline from Chale to Freshwater Bay and,

map continues on page 52

because of this, is under constant threat of erosion.

Opposite the pub driveway turn left onto the signposted sea-bound footpath, following New Chine on the left. Soon the path swings right along the clifftop, with the entire southwest coastline spread out ahead. About

Whale Chine

1.2km after leaving the road, follow the signposted footpath back to it and turn left.

The diversion is due to **Whale Chine**, a short distance ahead – 43m (140ft) deep and unusually bare of vegetation, it is by far the most impressive of the chines encountered on this walk, but not possible to cross. There is dispute over the origin of its name – a corruption of 'Wavell', perhaps, the name of the 16th- and 17th-century owners of nearby Atherfield Farm; or in memory of an 18th-century beached whale.

51

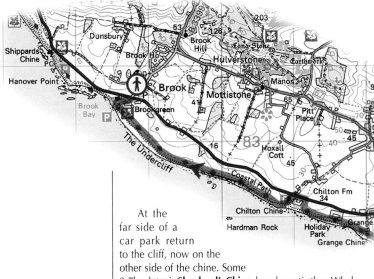

At the far side of a car park return to the cliff, now on the other side of the chine. Some 2.7km later is **Shepherd's Chine**, less dramatic than Whale Chine and navigable. Walk inland to find the descending path; turn left at the bottom beside the remains of a reservoir and pump house, and climb the steep slope at the end (or detour down steps for the beach).

Walk around the next chine (Cowleaze) and about 1km later swing right on a rise, with the village of Brighstone now visible. Shortly afterwards bear left to keep walking along the cliff. ◀ Soon after the Brighstone turn-off, descend and re-ascend **Grange Chine** to continue along the clifftop. Reach the incongruous Isle of Wight Pearl after 1km; it is said to house the largest collection of pearl jewellery in the UK, but walkers may be more attracted to the very welcome café, the only place for refreshments and shelter directly en route.

If you have had enough, or bus times are tight, after 1.4km go over two stiles in succession and continue up to Brighstone (under 30min walk away).

Make your way to the road behind the complex, turn left, cross over **Chilton Chine**, and return to the sea. Some 2.5km later, the path approaches the cottages at Brook Chine. At the cottages, follow a track leading to the road and bus stops at **Brook** (limited accommodation, pub at nearby Hulverstone). Alternatively, to continue along the Coastal Path turn left on a grassy path about 100 metres before the road.

WALK 4

Brook to Alum Bay

Start	Brook Chine, Brook
Finish	Needles Landmark Attraction, Alum Bay
Distance	11.9km (7.4 miles)
Grade	Moderate
Time	3hr
Refreshments	Freshwater Bay (5.1km), tearoom at Needles Old Battery (admission fee – 10.5km)
Public transport	To start: bus route 12; from finish: bus route 7
Parking	Car park at Brook Chine
Early finish	There are several opportunities up to Freshwater Bay to return to the coastal road (bus route 12, seasonal Island Coaster, and seasonal Needles Breezer at Freshwater Bay); alternatively the seasonal Needles Breezer at the Needles Batteries (10.2km)

If you are on the island for only a short time then, good weather permitting, this is one of the walks you shouldn't miss. Unlike the official Coastal Path, which curiously stops short on High Down before turning round to Alum Bay, this alternative carries on to the Victorian defence installations of the Old and New Batteries (National Trust) and remarkable viewpoints towards the famous Needles and Scratchell's Bay. The walk starts on the cliff tops above Compton Bay with the chalk cliffs of High Down drawing ever closer – look out for surfers and kitesurfers. Then, after Freshwater Bay, comes the ascent to the Tennyson Monument and the thrilling approach to 'the end of the island', a narrow peninsula with the sea on both sides. There is more clifftop walking after the about-turn and before the short final descent to The Needles Landmark Attraction on top of the cliffs of Alum Bay.

From the road junction at Brook Chine (limited accommodation, pub at nearby Hulverstone), follow footpath BS79 and turn left at a small car park to find the onward path. Note the contrast between the clay cliffs now underfoot

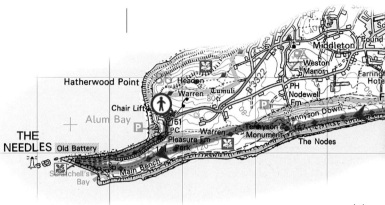

and the chalk cliffs of Tennyson Down and West High Down (collectively known as High Down) beyond. Continue walking on top of these beautiful but very fragile cliffs; in 900 metres pass through another car park at **Shippards Chine** overlooking Compton Bay.

> The cliffs above Compton Bay contain rocks which are up to 126 million years old, and the National Trust beach is the best place on the island to spot **dinosaur fossils** (at low tide). There are steps from the car park to the shore.

After a further 1.4km turn left before gates ahead to continue on top of the cliff. Soon skirt around narrow Compton Chine and ascend to the coastal road. Walk along the verge, but near the brow of the hill take the parallel path, soon descending seaward. On reaching a Victorian memorial to a dead child, take the left fork to continue towards **Freshwater Bay** (limited accommodation, hotel bar, cafés, shop, toilets); just before the final descent, bear left down steps to approach via its sea wall. At the bus stops on the other side of the bay turn left, and in 60 metres turn right to ascend Tennyson Down – although you may wish to detour to Fort Redoubt ahead.

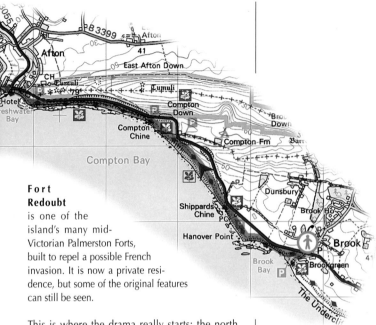

Fort Redoubt is one of the island's many mid-Victorian Palmerston Forts, built to repel a possible French invasion. It is now a private residence, but some of the original features can still be seen.

This is where the drama really starts: the north coast is soon visible as well as a wonderful view back towards Freshwater Bay and the entire Back of the Wight, and there is a sense of how wild and narrow the peninsula is becoming. Approaching the **Tennyson Monument**, look back for a new view over Freshwater. The monument is about 2km from Freshwater Bay – a good place to take stock and linger awhile.

The **Tennyson Monument**, with its granite cross, was erected in 1897 at the highest point of High Down in memory of the famous Poet Laureate who frequently left his Freshwater home (Farringford) to walk on this down, where the air, so he said, is 'worth sixpence a pint'. 'The Charge of the Light Brigade' is one work which was written on the down.

Tennyson Monument

Over to the right is Headon Warren, which is explored in Walks 5 and 15, and in clear conditions Bournemouth and the Isle of Purbeck are visible.

Strike out towards West High Down, always keeping to the centre of the ridge. ◀ Go through a gate about 2.3km from the monument to skirt clockwise around a transmitter and descend to a drive. Follow the sign opposite to the viewpoint – well worth the short detour for the view of **Scratchell's Bay** and **the Needles**.

The Needles are three separate rock towers off the island's westernmost point, and the most famous, distinctive and dramatic location on the island. There were originally four 'needles', and it is ironic that the only apparently needle-like rock of the four, known as 'Lot's Wife', was the one to collapse (in 1764). At one time the Needles were part of a chalk ridge that extended to Handfast Point near

The Needles

Swanage on the mainland, but the ridge had been all but eroded by 3000BC. The lighthouse on the furthest rock started operating on New Year's Day 1859 and has a 22.5km range. Since 1994 it has been – like all functioning British lighthouses today – very unromantically controlled by the General Lighthouse Authority in Harwich. Wind speeds at the Needles are often the strongest in the UK.

Return to the drive and turn left to walk towards the **New Battery** and its adjacent bus stop.

The **New Battery** was completed in 1895 as a replacement for the decaying Old Battery on the cliff below. Despite having some limited role in both world wars, it really came into its own between 1956 and 1971 as a site for testing firstly intercontinental ballistic missiles and then space rocket engines. There is an exhibition with limited opening hours.

Just shy of the bus stop, descend the adjacent concrete walkway towards the Old Battery – but instead of descending the penultimate flight of steps take a stony path and look down from the corner. Below mighty cliffs, and accessible only by sea, Scratchell's Bay is one of the most dramatic sights of the walk. ◄ Continue up the drive by the **Old Battery** entrance, the multi-shaded-cliffs of Alum Bay now ahead.

In season, frequent boat trips operate from Alum Bay to Scratchell's Bay via the Needles.

> The **Old Battery**, completed in 1863, was originally a Palmerston Fort, like Fort Redoubt. It saw action in both world wars, notably the second, when its guns were successful in destroying enemy torpedo boats and planes. The battery, which has a tearoom, is worth a visit if only for the 'secret tunnel' leading to a fantastic view of the Needles.

At the junction ahead turn left up steps to continue on a ledge. Pass concrete steps on the right after 200 metres. For the most dramatic approach to Alum Bay, drop down the grass (very steeply) 70 metres beyond these steps, on a path of sorts, to walk closer to the cliff edge. The path should not be dangerous, although care is needed due to potential erosion and possible strong winds. Once back on the drive, swing left to follow it down to **The Needles Landmark Attraction** above **Alum Bay** (bar, cafés, restaurant, shops, toilets, cable car). The bus stop is by the park entrance.

NORTH COAST

WALK 5
Alum Bay to Yarmouth

Start	The Needles Landmark Attraction, Alum Bay
Finish	Yarmouth
Distance	8.7km (5.4 miles)
Grade	Fairly easy
Time	2½hr
Refreshments	Totland Bay (2.6km), Colwell Bay (3.9km)
Public transport	To start: bus route 7 and seasonal Needles Breezer; from finish: bus route 7
Parking	Car park at The Needles Landmark Attraction
Early finish	Colwell (4.8km, bus route 7 and Needles Breezer). At no point is the route further than 30min from the main road (with bus stops)

One of the most consistently enjoyable stages of the Coastal Path, offering beauty and variety from start to finish. The climb up Headon Warren is rewarded with a spectacular view of the Needles and the start of the Solent. Then having descended to the sandy beach at Totland Bay, a lovely stretch of sea wall leads the walker to Colwell Bay: just as attractive, if slightly more shingly. Pleasant paths briefly head inland before the walker enters the delightful woodland of Fort Victoria Country Park and the final push to Yarmouth atop another sea wall.

From **The Needles Landmark Attraction** above **Alum Bay** (bar, cafés, restaurant, shops, toilets, cable car), follow the road east, and in 150 metres turn left onto a drive. In 100 metres, faced with three options, take the footpath on the right, with the Needles soon coming into view. In 350 metres, take the signposted footpath on the right, continuing the meandering ascent up**Headon Warren.** At

Sea wall, Totland Bay

a saddle (350 metres) bear half-right and ignore ways off the salient path until, in 200 metres, when a fence bars the way towards the Bronze Age burial mound ahead, turn left on an initially gradually descending path. Ignore ways off until a junction 400 metres from the previous one, where a signpost indicates a left fork. Exit Headon Warren along a stony path and turn left when deposited on a lane. In 200 metres, bear left down another stony path which leads down to the seafront at **Totland Bay** (café, toilets).

Turn right along the sea wall, soon passing **Totland Pier** – currently in a dilapidated state but scheduled to undergo restoration – and over a recent landslip to the huts at **Colwell Bay** (bar, cafés, shops, toilets). Just after the final set of huts, turn inland up steps, shortly turning right onto a track. turn left onto a drive. In 350 metres leave the track as it swings left for the footpath ahead, which emerges at a holiday park. Turn right

Hatherwood Point

Chair Lift

Alum Bay

141

Bench

in 70 metres, ignore ways off, and in a further 250 metres turn left onto another long drive. Just before the entrance to another holiday park (450 metres), turn right onto a signposted footpath and continue to border a lovely wildflower meadow. The path soon enters the mixed woodland of **Fort Victoria Country Park**.

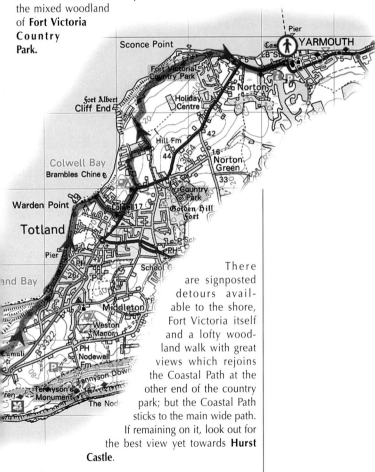

There are signposted detours available to the shore, Fort Victoria itself and a lofty woodland walk with great views which rejoins the Coastal Path at the other end of the country park; but the Coastal Path sticks to the main wide path. If remaining on it, look out for the best view yet towards **Hurst Castle**.

View to Hurst Castle

Fort Victoria was one of many Palmerston Forts built around the island to repel any French invasion, and was considered especially useful given the narrowness of the Solent here. The remains of the fort have been converted into an aquarium, planetarium, model railway and marine heritage centre. Detour along the road for 200 metres to reach it.

Hurst Castle served as the mainland's equivalent to Fort Victoria and Fort Albert, but was built 300 years earlier at about the same time as Yarmouth Castle. It hosted King Charles I on his final, fateful journey from Carisbrooke to London, as well as other 17th-century prisoners.

On reaching the road at the end of the country park, turn right, and in 90 metres bear left back into trees, almost immediately forking right to continue along the sea wall. In 450 metres it is tempting to continue alongside Norton Spit, but there is no through access, so instead join a road for the final short stretch, via a swing bridge over the Western Yar, into **Yarmouth** (limited accommodation, pubs, cafés, restaurants, shops, toilets).

WALK 6

Yarmouth to Shalfleet

Start	Yarmouth bus station/car park/ferry terminal
Finish	Shalfleet
Distance	12.7km (7.9 miles)
Grade	Easy
Time	3hr
Refreshments	None en route
Public transport	To start: bus route 7; from finish: bus route 7
Parking	Car park on A3054 just south of the bus station (on bend)
Early finish	No easy options beyond Bouldnor (1.6km)

A short stage but very lovely, and its relative remoteness will mean you will encounter very few other walkers. On the eastern edge of attractive Yarmouth, a short stretch of sea wall gives views towards Bouldnor Forest, soon to be explored. Beyond are the tiny, secluded hamlets of Cranmore and Hamstead, somewhat cut off from the rest of the island and surrounded by beautiful countryside. The path descends to a deserted stony beach and the western reaches of Newtown Harbour Nature Reserve before heading along woodland tracks and past a glorious waterside picnic spot just 20 minutes from Shalfleet.

From the car park at **Yarmouth** (limited accommodation, pubs, cafés, restaurants, shops, toilets), head north to the bus station and follow the Coastal Path sign into the town. Cross The Square to the left and turn right into High Street.

The High Street is sprinkled with distinguished 18th- and 19th-century houses and independent shops and restaurants. Its charm is humbler and somehow more genuine than, for instance, that of Godshill. At its end, descend Yarmouth Common to continue along the sea wall. Bouldnor Forest can now be seen. Just short of the very end of the wall, turn right up a wide, stony path and turn left at the road. In 450 metres take the signposted track left; at its end, a footpath branches into woodland – the start of **Bouldnor Forest.**

> The mixed woodland (Corsican pine is dominant) and red squirrel haven of **Bouldnor Forest** is under some threat due to coastal erosion eating away at Bouldnor Cliff (the forest's front line of defence). The cliff itself is immensely fossil-rich. In Victorian times there were plans to inhabit the area, including constructing a pier – which was begun and can be seen at low tide – but the unfavourable terrain proved too much of an impediment.

At a junction in 350 metres fork left to return back to the shoreline (momentarily). Then turn right at a T-junction just beyond a boardwalk and keep to the salient path as it ascends gradually through the forest. Bouldnor Battery, a coastal defence dating from the late 1930s, can soon be seen on the right. About 1.5km from the boardwalk, exit the forest and soon you are led out onto a stony track among several secluded properties in the hamlet of **Cranmore.**

Turn right to follow the track and left at a T-junction. In 250 metres turn right along the driveway of a new build, and continue on the footpath beyond, which shortly leads through a series of beautiful meadows. Some 700 metres from the new build, and having started

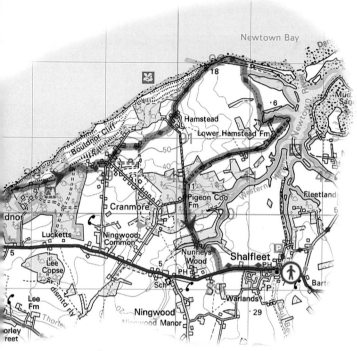

        to walk anti-clock-
      wise around a large field,
cross a stile on the second side. Turn left at a T-junction
with a track, which will bring you into the hamlet of
Hamstead.

    Continue past Hamstead Farm, gradually descend
back to the shoreline, and walk along the grassy path
behind the stony beach. ▶

    Shortly after the grassy path ends, turn right up steps
following the sign. (The Coastal Path does not rejoin the
sea again until near Cowes.) Cross the first of several
Newtown Harbour tributaries over a boardwalk to continue through a field with the harbour over on the left.
Keep to the right edge of another field and continue over
more boardwalks to head further into the nature reserve
and towards the harbour proper (see Walk 16 for more
information about Newtown Harbour).

Look out for a
memorial in the form
of a Celtic cross to
two young brothers
and a third man
who drowned near
here in the 1930s.

65

Ningwood Lake

On reaching a T-junction with a track, detour left briefly to admire one of the best views of the harbour. Then retrace your steps to continue along the track, and stay on it for the next 1.6km, where you turn left at a T-junction. In 200 metres ignore the prominent right fork, and in a further 700 metres – just beyond a bridge across Ningwood Lake with picture-perfect views either side – turn left into trees and, almost immediately, bear left off the main path, shortly passing an idyllic picnic spot.

Continue, then shortly turn left back on the main path, and turn left at the next fork as well (40 metres). Cross a stream and continue around two sides of a huge field to rejoin the Newport–Yarmouth road (A3054). Turn left along its grassy verge, soon reaching the end of the walk at the New Inn, **Shalfleet** (pub, shop).

WALK 7

Shalfleet to East Cowes

Start	New Inn, Shalfleet
Finish	Cowes or East Cowes
Distance	16.7km (10.4 miles)
Grade	Easy
Time	4hr
Refreshments	Thorness Bay Holiday Park (8.1km), Gurnard (12.7km and 13.7km)
Public transport	To start: bus route 7; from finish: bus route 1 (or routes 4, 5 and 9 from East Cowes, transferring by chain ferry)
Parking	Free car park in Mill Road, Shalfleet
Early finish	No easy options

The Coastal Path is something of a misnomer for most of this stage, as much of the coastline here is owned by the Ministry of Defence and, despite a minor deviation from the official route along footpaths, there is much unavoidable road-walking. But the roads are quiet and the sense of peace and tranquillity never disappears. Highlights are the beautiful isolated hamlet of Newtown, with its rich history; the clifftop walk between Thorness Bay and Gurnard offering expansive mainland views; and the final promenade stroll into Cowes. Outside summer, this stretch can be exceptionally muddy, even boggy, but waterproof footwear is essential at any time of year.

From the New Inn in **Shalfleet** (pub, shop), head up Mill Road, soon bearing right by the Coastal Path sign and crossing the Caul Bourne stream. On reaching a road turn left, but after 250 metres take a permissive path in the adjacent field. When you are led back onto the road, turn left up Town Lane. Cross a bridge at the point where a brook feeds into Causeway Lake and ascend to the hamlet of **Newtown** via its 17th-century Town Hall. ▶

Just past the National Trust car park and on the far side of the former town pub, turn right on a signposted

The Old Town Hall, built in 1699 and maintained by the National Trust, can be visited and suggests something of the town's past status (limited opening hours).

Newtown Town Hall

footpath to walk through a series of pretty meadows. Specifically: in 200 metres, go through a gate and turn right; ignore the narrow side-field, instead turning left just beyond it, towards a gate in the distance. Bear left at the start of the next field and continue ahead until reaching a lane – turn right.

Turn left at a T-junction (600 metres), cross Clamerkin Brook (650 metres) – another Newtown Harbour tributary – and after a further 250 metres deviate from the official Coastal Path by turning up Colemans Lane (this alternative uses paths instead of more roads to get to Porchfield). In 250 metres, turn left on 'hidden' footpath CB8, and on entering a second field stay near the right edge. Cross a stile in the far corner

to pick up CB7. Then, just after crossing a stile, turn immediately left and cross a lane to continue between two back gardens (CB6). Cross a stream, walk right, then sharp left across a field to cross a stile in its far corner. Continue past a farm to the road ahead, now in the hamlet of **Porchfield**.

map continues on
page 70

Turn right, now back on the official Coastal Path. In 550 metres, take the signposted footpath left and keep to the right-hand edge of four fields in succession, through some potentially

boggy ground. Exit the fourth field midway along, and turn left at the drive ahead. In 150 metres, turn right onto grass and right again when face-to-face with holiday homes. Follow Coastal Path signs through the **holiday park**, leaving it by way of a broad track which gradually descends to **Thorness Bay**, the grassy area by the shore-line making a perfect picnic spot.

Continue around the beach; midway around it, look out for a Coastal Path sign leading over a stile into a field. The route stays parallel to the bay but height is slowly gained, and there are soon sweeping views, first back to the west and then towards Gurnard. The path eventually ends at a lane back at sea level; turn left and cross a brook named Gurnard Luck, soon ascending with the road.

Turn left at the T-junction with Worsley Road; just after the first bend descend Winding Way back to the shore and the start of the long promenade at **Gurnard**. After 1km, the now-redundant lighthouse at **Egypt Point** is reached – the most northerly

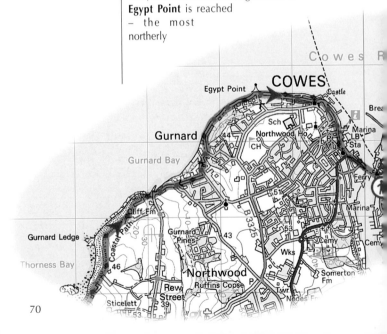

point on the island – and in a further 900 metres is **Cowes Castle**, home to the Royal Yacht Squadron. At the end of the promenade, turn up Watchbell Lane and then left towards the centre of **Cowes** (accommodation, supermarkets, pubs, cafés, restaurants, shops, toilets).

Cowes High Street

To carry on to East Cowes and the next stage of the Coastal Path, continue to the end of the high street and along Birmingham Road. Turn left at the end, which will lead to the Chain Ferry across the River Medina to **East Cowes** (small charge, cash only).

WALK 8

East Cowes to Ryde

Start	East Cowes (chain ferry)
Finish	Ryde Esplanade
Distance	12.7km (7.9 miles)
Grade	Fairly easy
Time	3hr
Refreshments	Wootton Bridge (6.9km), Fishbourne (8.5km), Quarr Abbey (9.2km)
Public transport	To start: bus routes 4 and 5 (or route 1 transferring by chain ferry); from finish: bus routes 2, 3, 4, 8 and 9, and train
Parking	There is a long-stay car park in Maresfield Road, East Cowes
Early finish	Whippingham (3.2km, bus routes 4 and 5), Wootton Bridge (6.9km, bus routes 4 and 9). At no point is the route further than 20min from the main road (with bus stops)

This section has even less coastal walking and even more roads than the previous one (indeed, the Solent is rarely even to be seen on this stretch). However, this is a mostly pretty walk, often among trees and with plenty of birdsong for company. The roads are mainly minor and quiet, usually with good views, and the walk deviates favourably from the official route by exiting East Cowes parallel to the River Medina and visiting Whippingham Church, designed partly by Prince Albert in Germanic style, with memorable views of the Medina from the approach. The increasingly popular – and quite magnificent – Quarr Abbey features later on: its church is considered one of the finest modern ecclesiastical buildings in Europe, and its peaceful gardens make a wonderful spot for a picnic.

From the chain ferry at East Cowes (limited accommodation, supermarkets, pubs, cafés, limited restaurants, shops, toilets), follow the Coastal Path sign past a chapel and

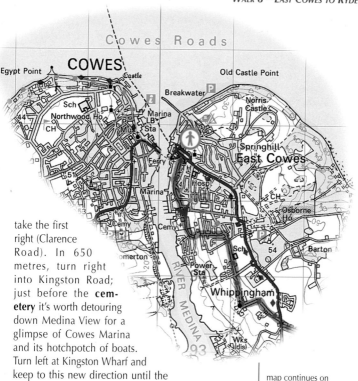

take the first
right (Clarence
Road). In 650
metres, turn right
into Kingston Road;
just before the **cem-
etery** it's worth detouring
down Medina View for a
glimpse of Cowes Marina
and its hotchpotch of boats.
Turn left at Kingston Wharf and
keep to this new direction until the
end of a footpath, turning right onto a road. The tower
and spires of **Whippingham Church** can soon be spotted;
keep heading towards it, now with a glorious view of the
Medina to the west.

map continues on
page 74

Whippingham Church was Queen Victoria and
Prince Albert's local church during their stays at
Osborne House. Their daughter Beatrice was mar-
ried and is buried here, as is the grandfather of Philip,
Duke of Edinburgh. The early medieval church was
rebuilt twice: first in 1804 by famous architect and
local John Nash (who went on to design London's
Regent Street and Regent's Park), and then in 1854

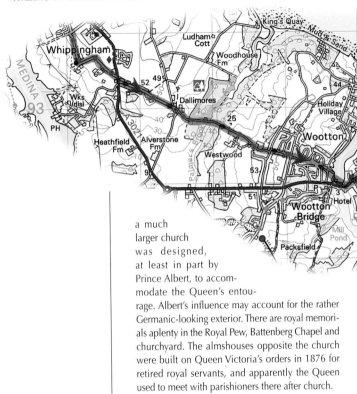

a much
larger church
was designed,
at least in part by
Prince Albert, to accom-
modate the Queen's entou-
rage. Albert's influence may account for the rather
Germanic-looking exterior. There are royal memorials aplenty in the Royal Pew, Battenberg Chapel and
churchyard. The almshouses opposite the church
were built on Queen Victoria's orders in 1876 for
retired royal servants, and apparently the Queen
used to meet with parishioners there after church.

Continue past the church to the main road at
Whippingham (small post office – limited opening – with
basic groceries), which is where the walk rejoins the official Coastal Path. Take Alverstoke Road to the right and
stay on this road to its end, in 2.3km; some cars use it
as a nicer alternative to the main road, but traffic is usually sporadic. Turn left onto Palmers Road and right into
Footways; at the T-junction take the footpath opposite
and keep following Coastal Path signs down to the Sloop
Inn at **Wootton Bridge** (limited accommodation, supermarket, pubs, restaurants, shops, toilets). Cross the bridge

between Old Mill Pond and the marina on Wootton Creek, and start ascending.

map continues on page 76

Wootton Creek has been in use since pre-Roman times, and there has also been a crossing here since time immemorial. It was this crossing that spawned the settlement of Wootton Bridge, which had traditionally been separate from Wootton up the (westerly) hill. Only recently have the two amalgamated to the extent that the names are often used interchangeably. Wootton was also the site of the 1969 Isle of Wight Festival, featuring Bob Dylan.

In 600 metres, turn left into Ashlake Copse Lane and keep to the current direction until, in 550 metres, you are led right (off the track). Turn left at a road, pass **Fishbourne** ferry terminal, and turn right opposite The Fishbourne pub a little further on. The imposing, red-brick **Quarr Abbey** will soon appear on the left; a visit to the Abbey and its tearoom in lovely gardens is highly recommended.

The present **Quarr Abbey** (pronounced 'cor') is so named because of an important nearby quarry mined since Roman times, which provided materials to build Winchester and Chichester cathedrals, and Winchester College. It was completed in 1912 to house a French Benedictine order, persecuted in their own country, which had moved to but subsequently outgrown Appuldurcombe House near Ventnor. Many of the original monks returned to France in 1922 and English monks moved in, but it took a further 15 years for the abbey to become independent. It is today still actively used and

Quarr Abbey

maintained by about 10 Benedictine followers. Check out the very comprehensive website (www. quarrabbey.org).

Some 300 metres to the east are the ruins of a **Cistercian abbey** constructed from 1132 and demolished in 1536 during the dissolution of the monasteries. In its heyday it was the foremost religious institution on the island and apparently served as a prison for Henry II's queen, Eleanor.

Some 900 metres beyond Quarr Abbey, branch left off the current path and turn left onto the lane at the end. Pass a very picturesque thatched cottage, then Binstead Church, to continue past **Ryde golf course** and up to (virtually) the main road. Follow the Coastal Path

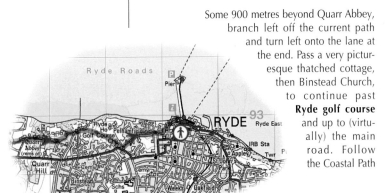

93

sign along a track – subsequently a road – for the next 750 metres, turning down Buckingham Road. Bear right at the bottom and turn left at the next T-junction past the Prince Consort Building to reach the esplanade at **Ryde** (accommodation, supermarkets, pubs, cafés, restaurants, shops, toilets).

Thatched cottage, Binstead

> The seaward facade of the colonnaded **Prince Consort Building** looks particularly elegant. Built in 1846 as a gift from Prince Albert to Queen Victoria, it was originally the home of the Royal Victoria Yacht Club, founded because the Royal Yacht Squadron at Cowes didn't allow female members!

WALK 9

Ryde to Sandown

Start	Ryde Esplanade Station
Finish	Sandown Pier
Distance	19.1km (11.9 miles)
Grade	Fairly easy (but the section through Priory Woods requires sure-footedness due to mud)
Time	5½ hr
Refreshments	Cafés and pubs are located every few miles throughout the walk
Public transport	To start: bus routes 2, 3, 4, 8 and 9, and train; from finish: bus routes 2, 3 and 8, and train
Parking	Long-stay car parks in St Thomas Street, just west of the pier
Early finish	At no point is the route further than a 20 min walk from bus stops (route 8). For those wishing to do this walk over two days, Bembridge Point is about half way and on the bus route.

In contrast to the previous two stages, the coastline is rarely left throughout this stage, yet walking stays beautiful and varied. From Ryde to the low-key village of Seaview the going is almost pancake-flat, but then the terrain gets slightly more challenging through muddy woods behind sublime Priory Bay Beach (a detour from the official Coastal Path to remain by the sea). Woods and beach end at the evocative St Helens Old Church, completely incongruous with its surroundings, and St Helens Duver, site of the island's first golf course. Bembridge Harbour is negotiated by way of a narrow causeway and the harbour road, built in the 1870s to connect St Helens to Bembridge over newly reclaimed land. The village centre of Bembridge is avoided; the route around the Foreland instead combines beach and sea wall walking with quiet lanes and footpaths lined with beautiful houses. A partly re-opened and well-restored long, wooded path takes the walker towards magnificent Whitecliff Bay from where there is a not too difficult ascent up Culver Down to the Lord Yarborough Monument and finally a dramatic descent towards Sandown.

From the esplanade at **Ryde** (accommodation, supermarkets, pubs, cafés, restaurants, shops, toilets), head east, soon passing some attractive Victorian villas, and continue following the coastline. Eventually, the walk enters the once private Appley Towers Estate, now pleasant parkland.

> Striking shoreside folly **Appley Tower** was erected in 1875 and used as a tea room for King George V and Queen Mary during their visits to owner Sir Hedworth Williamson.

At the café beside Puckpool Park, there is a choice of paths: through the park (converted from a land battery in 1928) or either of the parallel shore-side paths. All routes conjoin at the Boat House pub, the start of a 'suburb' of Seaview called **Spring Vale**. The five minute saunter round Hersey Nature Reserve, 650 metres from the pub, makes a pleasant detour. When the road turns inland, follow the Coastal Path sign through a gate to keep following the shoreline, soon emerging in the village of

map continues on
page 80

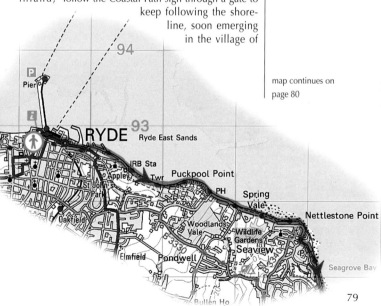

79

Seaview (limited accommodation, supermarkets, pubs, cafés, restaurants, shops, toilets).

Continue along Esplanade, past the yacht club, and ascend the high street. ◄ At the second crossroads, turn left onto Pier Road – or right to find bus stops beside the church – shortly returning to the shoreline.

At low tide, an even nicer alternative is to take the seawall path and walk a little way along a beach to rejoin the official route.

A very striking and unusual **pier** consisting of three suspension bridges stood here from 1881 to 1951 (when it was destroyed by a storm). It hosted ferries from Portsmouth and was complemented by a large hotel, a site now occupied by a block of flats with an original and tasteful design.

Follow signposts to pass some very individual and intriguing-looking houses. At **Seagrove Bay**, the walk deviates from the official Coastal Path (which can be followed in Walk 27). Follow the bay to its end, head up a flight of steps and descend onto the lovely sheltered beach at **Priory Bay** (some care may be needed here as the path was quite badly eroded at the time of writing). ◄ The beach is technically private for guests of a nearby hotel, but is a public right of way. Ascend a flight of steps near its end and turn left, soon following a yellow arrow down another flight of steps at the start of a very muddy path. Eventually, further flights of steps are ascended and descended in quick succession, and the route emerges on the southern section of Priory Bay Beach,

The Pitt Rivers Museum in Oxford houses Palaeolithic tools found on Priory Bay Beach which could be up to 700,000 years old.

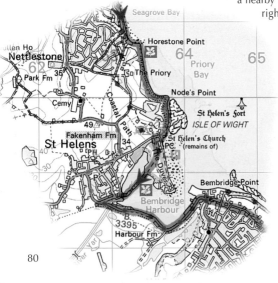

St Helen's Old Church

which is followed until its end at **St Helen's Old Church** and beach.

> **St Helen's Old Church** is a characterful old relic right on the seafront. The tower is all that remains of a 13th-century church that started disintegrating and fell out of use in Tudor times. In 1703 it was bricked up, and some years later was replaced by a new church further inland. Today it has no practical importance other than its white seaward side serving as an unusual seamark.

Turn sharp right at the church onto the tarmac, and at the T-junction turn left, now back on the official Coastal Path. Once past the Old Club House turn right at the first opportunity onto **St Helens Duver**, in the direction of the hill on the horizon.

> **Duver** is an island term for sand dune, and these former dunes, now National Trust land, were developed into the island's first golf course, at one time internationally renowned and played on by royalty and

map opposite continues on page 82

81

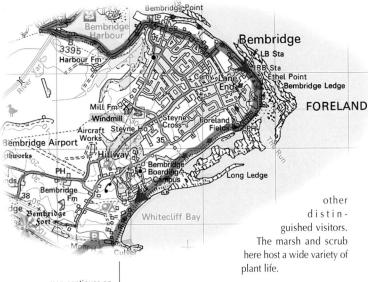

other
distin-
guished visitors.
The marsh and scrub
here host a wide variety of
plant life.

map continues on
page 85

Having reached the shore of **Bembridge Harbour**, which may or may not be filled with water depending on tide, continue through it on a delightful causeway; it is possible you will have just the seabirds for company.

Bembridge Harbour has been in use since pre-Roman times and originally penetrated southwest as far as Brading – the enlarged body of water being known as Brading Harbour or Brading Haven. The water was drained from the southwest part of the harbour in 1388 leaving mudflats, which were in turn reclaimed from the sea as late as 1878, eventually becoming today's Brading Marshes Nature Reserve. The resultant embankment, which you will soon walk along, provided a new route between Bembridge and St Helens and also carried the Brading to Bembridge railway branch line which operated from 1882 to 1953. It was from the harbour that Edward III set sail to invade Normandy in 1346, and it is said that it was the last stop for Nelson and his crew en route to the Battle of Trafalgar in 1805.

Round the bends at the end of the causeway and bear left at Mill House. Bear left at the road ahead and at the T-junction turn left onto Embankment Road. The Eastern Yar is soon crossed, almost at its mouth, and keep a look out for the harbour's idiosyncratic houseboats some way along. The embankment road ends at **Bembridge Point**. To detour to the point itself (recommended), continue to the end of Beach Road opposite the pub. Visible here as a white structure to the left is **St Helens Fort**.

View from Bembridge Point

An outing is arranged every summer, when the tide is particularly low, to view **St Helens Fort** from St Helen's Old Church. Other Spithead forts are seen during this walk. They were built as defences in mid-Victorian times to repel a French invasion that never came, and have become known as Palmerston Forts (or Follies) after the relevant Prime Minister.

Back on the 'main' road, follow the Coastal Path sign due east, and turn left at a T-junction with a lane. Maintain the current direction along a footpath after the tarmac ends and turn left just before Swains Lane. At the sea, descend steps to continue along the beach, follow

Beach at Whitecliff Bay

The Bembridge Lifeboat Station was established in 1867. It currently has two lifeboats and is open daily for visitors.

a sea wall after 300 metres, and continue past the RNLI shop and pier. ◄ In 130 metres, it is recommended to deviate slightly from the official Coastal Path by descending steps and continuing on the curved beach around the **Foreland**, the eastern vertex of the island.

When the direction becomes southwesterly, with a change in view, follow the sea wall now visible. Ascend steps after 500 metres and turn left (or right to shortly find a pub). Maintain the current direction along a recently re-opened path above badly eroded cliffs. Further along, the path has recently been resurfaced, so the thick mud which used to plague this route is now a thing of the past. Ignore ways off to eventually emerge into the open, facing long rows of holiday homes at **Whitecliff Bay**. Turn left, following the Coastal Path sign, to pass these holiday homes above the wide, sandy beach. Eventually, start an ascent of **Culver Down** and continue on the clear path up to the **Lord Yarborough Monument** at the top. The weather can be tempestuous up here – as on all exposed high ground on the island – but on a clear day the view stretches beyond Bembridge Airport and Harbour, over the Spithead to and beyond Portsmouth. Savour the moment and keep an eye out for light aircraft landing.

Erected in 1849, the 104m (341ft) **Lord Yarborough Monument** commemorates the memory of Charles Anderson-Pelham, 1st Earl of Yarborough, Lincolnshire MP, and island notable by virtue of being the first Commodore of Cowes' Royal Yacht Squadron, marrying into the Worsley family, and consequently coming to own Appuldurcombe House. The monument was originally placed where Bembridge Fort is now, but was relocated here on construction of the fort.

Turn right onto the tarmac drive ahead, immediately bearing left and taking in a new, equally impressive, southerly view (of Sandown Bay). Continue to follow the sea

Towards Sandown

above the cliffs towards Sandown, the most stunning stretch of coastline walking on the east of the island. In terms of fossil spotting the beach below is second only to Compton Bay. Having descended to the car park at **Yaverland**, walk along the beach or promenade to reach the pier at **Sandown** (accommodation, supermarkets, pubs, cafés, restaurants, shops, toilets).

> **Sandown Pier** is the only functioning pleasure pier on the island. Looking at its rather subdued state today, it is hard to believe that in its heyday it hosted such distinguished guests as the Queen and Lord Mountbatten (penultimate island Governor), and entertainers including Harry Secombe, Bob Monkhouse and Lenny Henry, as well as providing ferry services to Portsmouth. The pier was built in 1876 and subsequently much refurbished. Entertainment was provided at a pavilion at the shore end of the pier; before being reconstructed in 1968, it boasted an incredible 980 seats.

WEST WIGHT

The Long Stone (Walks 12 and 13)

WALK 10

Shorwell circular

Start/Finish	Crown Inn, Shorwell
Distance	16km (10 miles)
Grade	Moderate
Time	4hr
Refreshments	None en route
Public transport	Bus route 12 (limited service). A car is ideal transport as buses run only every 2 or 3 hours, but if you have long to wait in Shorwell you could always repair to the pub.
Parking	B3323 or Crown Inn car park (customers only)
Early finish	Newport–Shorwell road (B3323) (7.3km and 9.3km, bus route 12)

The downland to the immediate northwest and northeast of Shorwell is off the beaten track even for walkers, yet is surprisingly appealing and makes for a wonderful outing if the weather stays good. The first stage leads up onto Limerstone Down, but then instead of going through Brighstone Forest the walk heads onto the plateau of Cheverton Down, descends to a very remote valley and meanders through the deciduous woodland of Rowborough Bottom. Back on the Newport to Shorwell road the walk continues with an ascent of Chillerton Down and draws closer towards its mighty transmitter, a significant landmark that can be seen across the island. The approach back to Shorwell is delightful, and highlights the extent of the woodland surrounding the village.

From the Crown Inn at **Shorwell** (limited accommodation, pub, shop) walk west along the road and in 200 metres abruptly right on bridleway SW6 opposite a very elegant detached house. Beyond the gate ahead ascend half-left through the field ignoring ways off the faint path. Having crossed into another field, continue on a grassy path – look back to see Shorwell behind you.

In 150 metres bear right onto a ledge, parallel to Limerstone Down to the north (which will be climbed shortly). Stay on the ridge, eventually walking above two sides of a vast field (exit the field at the first corner reached) and ascending to field gates in the distance. Keep ignoring ways off this final stage of ascent, but look down to observe the convoluted topography of the low hills around Brighstone.

On the ridge near the top of **Limerstone Down** turn right. Make a short detour to the toposcope at the top where, naturally, the best view yet awaits. Then continue on the track until you are level with barns away to the left (300 metres). Here, turn left through a field gate (there may be a white arrow on the fencepost) and continue anti-clockwise around the field perimeter which may be very overgrown, but passable, in summer. Swing right with the fence some way along the second side, and then again after 300 metres. At the field corner, turn right and then left at the junction ahead, along a wide stony track – now on **Cheverton Down** and facing Chillerton Down across the valley (which will be climbed later). In 1.2km turn left down an equally broad track. Fork right after 150

Rowborough Bottom

metres to continue the descent, now on a grassy path, to the floor of the remote valley. Turn right, shortly entering the woodland of Rowborough Bottom. Stay on the main track through the wood – a beautiful stroll.

In 1.3km – or about 150 metres before the just-visible Newport–Shorwell road (B3323) – turn left on an ascending track. ◄ When the track eventually swings left, turn right through a gate to descend to the road, which marks the end of the longest and most strenuous half of the walk. Bus stops are to the north, but the onward route takes N137a, almost opposite.

Turn right onto N146 at a junction in 750 metres, at the foot of an incline, and branch right into woodland in a further 80 metres. The path shortly leaves the wood to

To end the walk early, continue to the road and turn right for bus stops.

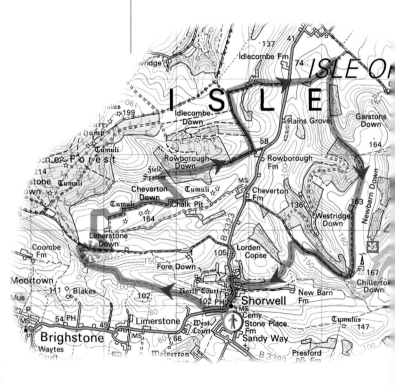

Atop Chillerton Down

ascend **Chillerton Down**. On reaching the top, continue between rows of conifers.

Eventually the trees are left behind and vistas open up west and east. Pass an isolated barn – somewhere to shelter if caught up in a storm – and plough on towards the slender and quite awe-inspiring 230m (755ft) transmitter.

> It could be argued that the **transmitter** complements – rather than detracts from – the stark beauty of the landscape. The most visually prominent landmark on the island, it was built in 1958, used for television until 1985, and currently broadcasts local FM and DAB radio.

At the T-junction just beyond it, go right, the Back of the Wight coastline now visible again.

In 850 metres, look out for, and turn left on, a broad stony track. Immediately past a cattle grid with **New Barn Farm** ahead, bear right and near the top of the short ascent, branch left on a faint grassy path (the higher of the two possible options), soon with lovely belts of trees on both sides. Midway through the next field, branch

Thatched rooftops of Shorwell

right on a faint path leading into trees. On entering the woodland, almost immediately turn left at a T-junction of sorts, and in 80 metres cross the wooden footbridge over Shorwell Shute, which those travelling from Newport would have spotted earlier.

Once over the bridge turn left, and left again on the drive below – although do detour right briefly to see the entrance to Jacobean **North Court**, one of the village's three manor houses (West Court and Wolverton Manor, both slightly older, are the other two). Back on the road, turn right to continue past the village shop and church to arrive back at the Crown Inn in **Shorwell**.

WALK 11

Shorwell to Niton

Start	Crown Inn, Shorwell
Finish	Niton
Distance	14km (8.8 miles)
Grade	Moderate
Time	3½hr
Refreshments	None en route
Public transport	To start: bus route 12; from finish: bus route 6
Parking	B3323 or Crown Inn car park (customers only)
Early finish	Near Chale (8.1km, bus route 6)

There are two distinct parts to this walk, which links two of the main villages on the south of the island. The first is low key and remote but still lovely and varied, meandering through empty, atmospheric fields and woods near to, but just out of sight of, the sea. After crossing the Newport–Chale road, the second part of the route ascends St Catherine's Down and visits both the Hoy Monument and St Catherine's Oratory Lighthouse, the latter with stupendous views. Pick a sunny day for this walk.

From the Crown Inn at **Shorwell** (limited accommodation, pub, shop) walk west along the road and in 250 metres turn left on footpath SW3. Follow the faint path half-right, and having crossed into another field, immediately turn right. Start walking anti-clockwise around the next field to cross a stile in the second corner. Cross a stream and continue over wooden planks through a wood. At a path junction opposite a house turn right, then almost immediately left over a footbridge to continue on concrete.

This is the estate of **Wolverton Manor**. The manor house, on the left, is a late Tudor property with 18th-century additions, and is still a private residence.

93

Wolverton Manor

Maintain your current direction at a lane, and at the next junction turn left, then right shortly after on a sign-posted bridleway. After a short, sharp ascent, continue on the initially pathless grass and, just after crossing a hedgerow, turn right to walk along the right edge of this field and the next, at the end of which turn left and shortly right through a gate. You will soon be climbing St Catherine's Down, visible in the distance.

At a T-junction with a concrete track (800 metres) turn right, then after 250 metres take SW21 through the centre of a huge field. In 350 metres, walk to the left of the hedgerow ahead to keep to the right of a new field, then in 250 metres turn right over two stiles and continue towards the right of the hillock ahead. Keep to the left of two fields – the path resumes at the foot of the hillock in the second field. At the end of this second field, turn right to locate the entrance to the next field. Cross a stream (200 metres) and immediately turn left. Having crossed the stream a second time, almost immediately bear half-right at the start of the field ahead on a faint path. On reaching a barbed wire fence turn left, heading towards a house in the distance. Ignore ways off, then just before the isolated house seen earlier, turn right (C28). Ignore ways off to walk through a lovely stretch of woodland and past late 17th-century **Pyle Manor**. At a road junction continue on Southdown, then almost immediately turn left on C23 steeply uphill, turning left at the top, now with a clear view of both the Hoy Monument (left) and St Catherine's Oratory (right) on St Catherine's Down ahead.

On reaching a lane turn right then shortly left (C20). Cross a

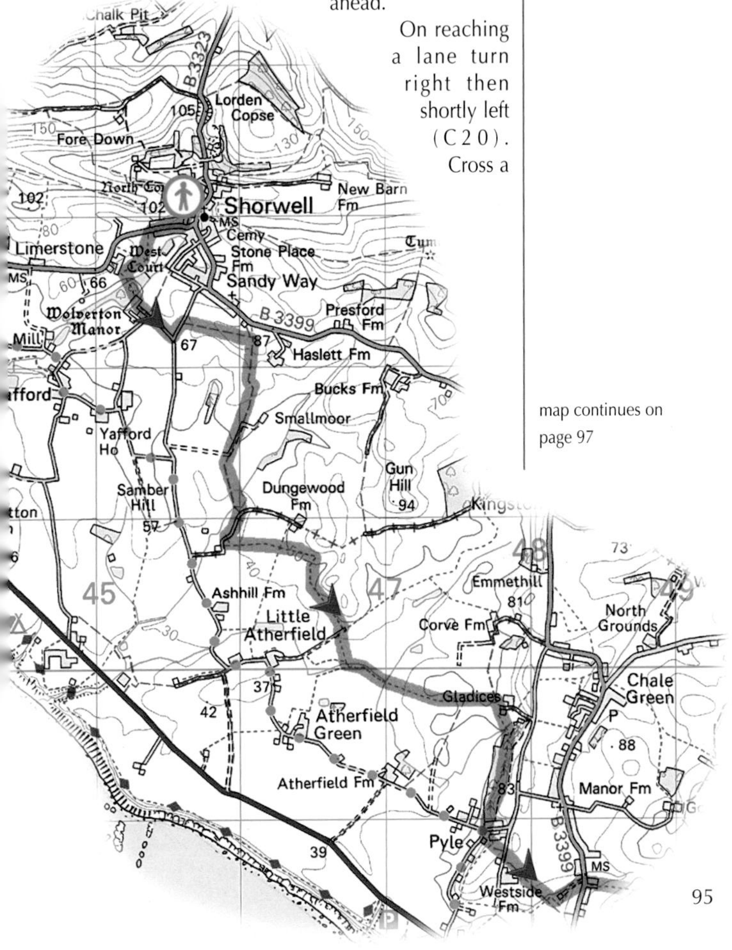

map continues on page 97

95

stream after 400 metres, then immediately turn left. On reaching a building on the left, bear half-right through the field to reach the Newport–Chale road (B3399). ◀

Cross the road to take C4. Keep near the right edge of two fields and the left edge of the next three. Bear left round a hillock, then shortly take a path up the steep grassy embankment on the left. Cross a stile to continue along the bottom of the escarpment, soon with a comprehensive 180-degree view from the Back of the Wight to the mainland. In 350 metres cross a stile on the right; then at a path junction after 450 metres, turn right along a signposted bridleway. After 250 metres go sharp right on C6 to ascend to the **Hoy Monument**.

> The 22m (72ft) **Hoy Monument** was erected by trader Michael Hoy to commemorate a visit to England by Tsar Alexander I in 1814, although ironically there is a plaque commemorating British losses (against Russian forces) in the Crimean War on the southern side. There is something rather lonely and melancholic about the monument's location, somewhat enclosed on three sides of a

If you don't feel like tackling St Catherine's Down, bus stops are about 50 metres on the right.

Hoy Monument

narrow ridge: quite the obverse to the spectacular vista from the nearby Pepper Pot.

Walk south along the grassy plateau, soon with a marvellous view east (the large village is Whitwell). Take either fork whenever the path divides, then beyond a gate, bear half-left and turn right at a fence to ascend **St Catherine's Hill** and eventually reach **St Catherine's Oratory Lighthouse**.

St Catherine's Oratory Lighthouse (affectionately called the 'Pepper Pot' for obvious reasons) has more visitors than the Hoy Monument to the north, being better known and more easily accessible. Situated on top of St Catherine's Hill – at 236m (774ft) one of the highest points

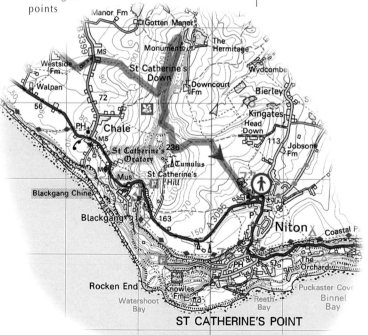

on the island – it was completed in 1328 by a landowner who was ordered by church courts to build it as punishment for stealing (or receiving stolen) French wine. Solitary monks used to man the lighthouse until the adjoining oratory was demolished during the Dissolution of the Monasteries. An increasing number of shipwrecks led to work commencing on a new lighthouse close by in 1785, but only the foundation stones are visible (below the radio mast and nicknamed the Salt Pot), as it was never completed. Instead the decision was made to build the current gleaming St Catherine's Lighthouse on the southern tip of the island (see Walk 24).

Almost opposite the entrance to the lighthouse is a white trig point; go through the swing gate beside it to continue across the field, with a sensational view. Notice your destination (Niton) down on the right. Go through a gate and bear quarter-left on a faint path, shortly skirting around a hollow on the right, and then turning right on a wide grassy path just shy of the fence below. Go through a gate and continue on an enclosed path. Just past two gates and a stile (250 metres) turn right on a track which will descend all the way to the Norman church at **Niton** (shops, toilets). Turn left for the shops and bus stops.

WALK 12
Brighstone circular

Start/Finish	Three Bishops pub, Brighstone
Distance	13.3km (8.3 miles)
Grade	Moderate
Time	3hr
Refreshments	Mottistone Manor Garden (admission fee – 8.3km)
Public transport	Bus route 12 (limited service)
Parking	Warnes Lane car park (behind the Three Bishops pub)
Early finish	Mottistone (8.3km, bus route 12), Military Road (9.4km and 12.3km, seasonal Island Coaster)

This is a walk of great contrasts, featuring open downland, deep forest, coast path, and a liberal scattering of wonderful views. The 4km middle section passes through Brighstone Forest, and to walk through it can be quite a humbling experience; there are few sounds other than birdsong, route-finding is straightforward, and fellow walkers are few and far between – perfect for long conversation or solitary contemplation. The route descends to the Long Stone – arguably the most important prehistoric monument on the island – before arriving at Mottistone, with its lovely church and manor house and garden. The walk may be cut short here, but it would be a shame to miss the clifftop stretch back to Brighstone.

From the Three Bishops pub at **Brighstone** (limited accommodation, pub, restaurant/café, shops, toilets), walk towards the newsagent and turn right up North Street, one of the island's most unashamedly olde-worlde streets with its cute library and museum. Cross the T-junction ahead to continue on bridleway BS81. In 400 metres, branch left off the path to come out into the open, and immediately turn right to ascend steeply on a grassy path. At the top of the steep incline bear left, still ascending, now with a wonderful vista of Brighstone and the sea.

At a crossroads of grassy paths in 100 metres, go right, shortly descending beside the edge of a field. The majestic spectacle of Limerstone Down is ahead; soon you will be walking along its ridge. At the T-junction on the valley floor, take the lower of the two adjacent parallel paths on the right. Stay on this enclosed path until another T-junction is reached and turn left to ascend **Limerstone Down**. A truly stunning view soon appears, encompassing the eastern coastline of the Isle of Purbeck on a clear day. At the top of the down, cross the track to continue on BS8 within **Brighstone Forest**.

The sprawling, predominantly broadleaved **Brighstone Forest** is the island's largest, although Parkhurst is a very close second. Planted only in the middle of the 20th century, it nevertheless has

North Street, Brighstone

something of a mystical air about it, and walking through it is always a pleasure. There is frequent felling, but conservation work is underway to diversify the forest's (currently mainly beech) content and improve conditions for the red squirrel population.

Bear left after 200 metres, and at a crossroads (150 metres) turn left onto a broad track. Cross the Tennyson Trail and take the descending track opposite, deeper into the forest. Cross a road (1.4km) and continue on CB17. After a further 1km cross over a path crossroads, and in a further 850 metres take a left fork to finally emerge from the forest. Immediately beyond a Tennyson Trail signpost and dual-coast view (60 metres), turn left on a hidden bridleway. Stay on the ridge – the view of woodland, downs and sea is the finest so far and one of the most aesthetically pleasing on the entire island.

At a junction after 600 metres, bear right through a metal gate to continue your descent. At a T-junction turn left, shortly reaching the 5000-year-old **Long Stone** (see Walk 13). Walk around the monument on the stony track and in 350 metres turn sharp right on a wide grassy path (about a 330-degree turn). Then on a left bend in a further 350 metres, turn left through a kissing gate onto a path that meanders through pretty woodland. Ignore ways off the salient path, eventually arriving at the village of **Mottistone**. The manor house and bus stops are to the left.

The name **Mottistone** probably comes from the alternative name for the Long Stone ('Moot Stone'). The village's manor house was mentioned in the *Domesday Book*, but the current house is Tudor in origin and was originally home to the Cheke family. One resident, Sir John Cheke, was tutor to King Edward VI. The house was restored in 1926 by a notable island family, the Seelys, or to be precise the first Baron Mottistone, and the family bequeathed the estate to the National Trust in 1963. It is still lived in by family members, and currently opened to the public for guided tours one day a year. The beautiful gardens, however, are open most days and well worth a visit. Mottistone Church is

Mottistone Church

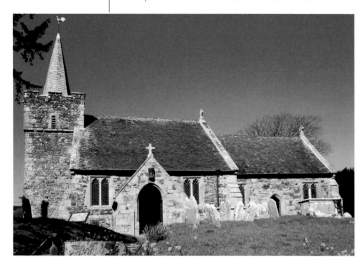

Back towards Brighstone

12th century in origin, with substantial 15th-century and Victorian additions and alterations.

To continue to Brighstone, take Church Lane near the bus stops and continue into Ridget Lane, which becomes a track leading down to the coastal road; cross the road to reach the sea and turn left on the Coastal Path. On reaching **Chilton Chine** turn inland and re-cross the coast road to continue on BS71. On reaching concrete continue in your current direction past **Chilton Farm**, then just before a left bend take BS62 on the right. Cross Galley Lane (1km) and continue on BS24. Turn right on a residential road, then almost immediately left on BS25 back to the Three Bishops in **Brighstone**.

WALK 13

Brighstone to Yarmouth

Start	Three Bishops pub, Brighstone
Finish	Yarmouth
Distance	13.3km (8.3 miles)
Grade	Moderate
Time	3hr
Refreshments	None en route
Public transport	To start: bus route 12; from finish: bus route 7
Parking	Warnes Lane car park (behind the Three Bishops pub)
Early finish	Thorley (10.3km and 11.2km, bus route 7)

A pleasant meander through the surprisingly sizeable outskirts of Brighstone leads into Grammars Common – a beautiful, solitary hillside wood, which is likely to linger in the memory. The walk descends and re-ascends to the Long Stone – some 5000 years old – following which a balcony path provides stunning views of the Back of the Wight. After passing Grade II listed Shalcombe Manor, the walk takes on a different feel as it heads north through the rolling fields of lonely rural West Wight. After a second beautiful wood, Mill Copse, the walk emerges at the Western Yar and travels beside it the short distance into Yarmouth.

From the Three Bishops pub in **Brighstone** (limited accommodation, pub, restaurant/café, shops, toilets), walk towards the newsagent and turn right up pretty North Street, with its small library and museum. Turn left at the T-junction and in 550 metres left again (footpath BS38). Turn right at a lane and in 150 metres turn left on 'hidden' BS39. Reaching another road turn right and continue on the path at the end of the road. Turn left on a path between animal enclosures (just before the current path also swings left), which will twist and turn until eventually you are following a farm drive. A short way along turn right (BS66) and ascend, soon with the

ubiquitous but always delightful sea view, and Brighstone now below and behind you.

Soon enter Grammars Common, a mainly coniferous wood idyllically situated. Bear left at the initial fork to continue to a path T-junction. Turn right to remain inside the wood, with a view now to High Down. Turn left at the next T-junction to continue the ascent deeper into the wood. Eventually the path exits the wood and heads between gorse bushes into a small but lovely grassy glade. At its end swing left and descend to a lane. Turn right, and then left after 70 metres (BS84) to continue up to the **Long Stone**.

Path up to the Long Stone

The **Long Stone** is actually two stones of iron sandstone, the larger 4m (13ft) high, which formed the eastern end of a Neolithic burial mound – or long barrow – constructed some 5000 years ago. The form of the barrow can still be made out behind the stones. Its significance as a meeting place led to the Saxons calling it the Moot Stone, which, it is believed, led to the naming of the nearby village of Mottistone.

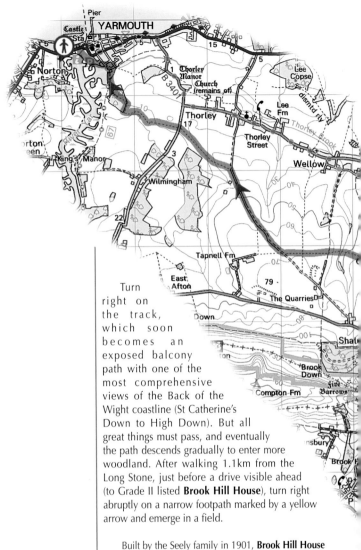

Turn right on the track, which soon becomes an exposed balcony path with one of the most comprehensive views of the Back of the Wight coastline (St Catherine's Down to High Down). But all great things must pass, and eventually the path descends gradually to enter more woodland. After walking 1.1km from the Long Stone, just before a drive visible ahead (to Grade II listed **Brook Hill House**), turn right abruptly on a narrow footpath marked by a yellow arrow and emerge in a field.

Built by the Seely family in 1901, **Brook Hill House** was subsequently leased by JB Priestley, author of *An Inspector Calls*. The house is situated in a commanding hillside position (there are excellent views of it from the coast and Compton Down), but its current function as an apartment block does not really do justice to its romantic setting. The house is not to be confused with Brook House, the Seelys' older residence, situated in the hamlet of Brook itself, towards the coast.

Descend half-left across the pathless grass to a road not yet visible (this can be quite an ordeal in summer when the grass is long), with the tortoise-shell figure of Brook Down rising ahead. Turn right and after 550 metres go left onto S21 to continue uphill, with **Shalcombe Manor** (also Grade II listed) and its pond hidden on your right. Continue between hedgerows to a road. Cross and continue on the field path ahead, shortly with a good view

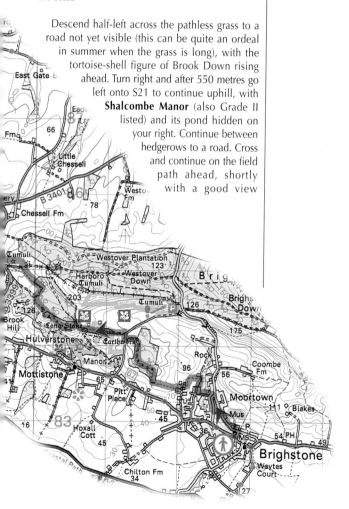

towards Newtown Harbour and the extensive woodland to its west.

Go through a gate (200 metres) and bear half-left across the field to the far corner. Shortly walk along the edge of a vast third field, but after about 400 metres keep your eyes peeled for a stile on the right. Don't cross it, but take the path left across the field. Descend to cross a stream, re-ascend through another field, and stay in this predominantly westerly direction until a lane is reached. Turn right and stay on the lane for the next 1.2km, where you turn left onto Y1 – a lovely path initially beside saplings. ◀

To end the walk early, continue along the lane into the village of Thorley to find bus stops just to the right.

Remain on Y1 after it crosses a road (further bus stops are at the junction to the right). In 1.1km the path enters Mill Copse, an ancient woodland site containing a high proportion of 1960s conifers. As with other woods on the island, broadleaf trees have recently been planted to replace many of the conifers, and this trend is likely to continue. Bear right at the immediate main fork and ignore ways off the salient path to exit the wood and continue towards the Western Yar estuary. Cross a track – the former Newport–Freshwater railway line – to stay on Y1, and just past the 18th-century mill (see Walk 14), bear left to stay beside the Yar. Skirt around the near side of the car park to emerge opposite the bus station at **Yarmouth** (limited accommodation, pubs, cafés, restaurants, shops, toilets).

Yarmouth Mill

WALK 14

Best of eastern Freshwater (circular)

Start/Finish	Yarmouth bus station/car park/ferry terminal
Distance	11.2km (7 miles)
Grade	Easy
Time	2½hr
Refreshments	Central Freshwater (4.1km), Freshwater Bay (5.9km), Freshwater Old Village (8.5km)
Public transport	Bus route 7
Parking	Car park on A3054 just south of the bus station (on bend)
Early finish	Central Freshwater (4.1km, bus route 7), Freshwater Bay (5.9km, bus route 12 and seasonal Needles Breezer)

This enjoyable and unchallenging figure of eight walk is especially ideal for day-trippers arriving on the Lymington ferry. From charming Yarmouth – the smallest town in the UK – the walk follows the course of a former railway line beside the serene Western Yar estuary, with views over to Freshwater village and Tennyson Down beyond. Beautiful Afton Marsh follows, and walkers arrive surprisingly quickly in Freshwater Bay on the opposite coast of the island, with classic views towards the mighty cliffs of High Down. Back inland, quiet paths and country lanes lead up to the old village of Freshwater, with its church, pub and quaint houses. Finally a pretty route through fields and woodland heads back onto the coastal road in Yarmouth.

From the bus station in **Yarmouth** (limited accommodation, pubs, cafés, restaurants, shops, toilets) head inland to the car park, and at its far side turn left on the grass to start walking beside the Western Yar estuary, shortly reaching a mill.

> The **mill** was built in 1793 to replace a 17th-century wooden one – which was itself built so that ships no longer had to continue east to Thorley on an increasingly unnavigable channel. After the

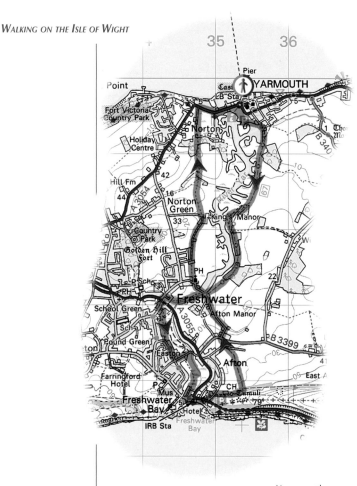

Yarmouth Harbour breakwater was constructed in the 1840s the mill fell into disuse. More recently, it was owned and resided in by renowned 20th-century historian AJP Taylor.

Just past the mill turn left on footpath Y2 to reach what was Yarmouth Station, complete with original

platform, and turn right on the former railway track to continue beside the estuary, staying on it for the next 2.7km.

The old Yarmouth Station

The **Western Yar** river today is just 4 miles long, but used to be much longer; the depletion of its sources over the centuries accounts for its disproportionately large estuary. The estuary – the epitome of rural tranquillity – is replete with a huge array of resident and migrating birds, such as curlew, dunlin, redshank, Brent goose, teal and widgeon, and has a secure conservation status. The saltmarshes developed after Yarmouth Harbour's breakwater was built in 1847, thus slowing down the flow of the river; ongoing erosion of the marshes is a problem, however.

Many of the birds that visit the Western Yar travel thousands of miles and rest here on their journey, no doubt replenishing their energy on the abundance of small sea life breeding on the mudflats. Look out too for red squirrels when the bridleway becomes tree-lined.

The track ends at a junction with a country lane beside a stone bridge – a lovely spot and the centre of the walk's figure of eight, so it will be visited again. Cross the bridge, then immediately turn left (F58). Walk through the marshland, which is potentially swampy at first. Emerging on a road in **Freshwater** (limited accommodation, supermarkets, pub, café, restaurants, shops, toilets), turn left at the T-junction ahead. Pass the site of the former Freshwater Station on the left – the terminus for trains from Newport via Yarmouth – to continue on Stroud Road. ◄ After 120 metres turn left (F37), shortly passing through a truly idyllic garden (only the path is public, unfortunately).

Turn right here for bus stops.

Ignore path offshoots; on reaching a lane turn left, and at its end go left again. After 200 metres turn right beside a sign for Afton Marsh Nature Reserve (ignore the Freshwater Way signpost shortly before). Turn left at a T-junction to continue beside the marsh – another very beautiful area. Emerge onto a gravel road, and almost immediately turn left on F52, shortly turning right into a car park, now in **Freshwater Bay** (limited accommodation, hotel bar, cafés,

Western Yar, with Freshwater Church in the background

112

Freshwater Church

shop, toilets). Cross the road and continue to the seafront, turning left along the sea wall. ▸

Climb the steps at the end of the sea wall and immediately turn inland. Re-cross and ascend the coastal road and take the first left (Southdown Road), shortly bearing right on F32. In 350 metres bear left, still on F32, with the sea just visible in three directions at this junction. Keep a hedgerow on your left and bear left at the corner of the golf course (F31). At a T-junction turn right and cross the road to continue on The Causeway. Shortly after the bend, look behind for a view towards East Afton Down; on this hill in 1970, hundreds of thousands of people congregated to watch the Isle of Wight Festival, featuring Jimi Hendrix, The Doors, Joni Mitchell and numerous other A-list acts.

Soon cross the stone bridge you crossed earlier and stay on this country lane up to **Freshwater Old Village** and its church.

The **Church of All Saints** dates from the 7th century, although it has of course been heavily restored since then, mainly in early medieval and Victorian times. The interior contains several

It is possible to end the walk here – bus stops are to the right.

113

Tennyson memorials, and several members of the family – although not the great man himself – have been laid to rest in the churchyard. The huge yew tree to the right is possibly the oldest tree on the whole island.

Take F1 beside the church wall; notice the amusing anecdote (and associated sculpture) about a drunk 19th-century smuggler. Soon continue ahead on concrete. Just before a farm driveway turn left through a field gate, then immediately right. Ignore path offshoots until, in 650 metres, the route bears right through a wooden gate, continuing to follow the Freshwater Way.

Keep to the left of the field ahead, and to the right of the next. Shortly after entering a wood turn left at a T-junction along a track to reach a road. Here, turn right to return to the **Yarmouth** bus station via the swing bridge.

Freshwater is, technically, almost an island itself, and at one time crossings of the Yar could be made only by ferry. A **bridge** linking Yarmouth and Freshwater was constructed in 1863, charging a toll, and was replaced with the present one in 1987, which opens for 10min every hour to accommodate vessels (they have right of way at all other times as well).

WALK 15

Best of western Freshwater (circular)

Start/Finish	Vine Inn, School Green Road, Freshwater
Distance	16.3km (10.2 miles)
Grade	Moderate
Time	4½hr
Refreshments	Colwell Bay (3.2km), Totland Bay (4.4km), The Needles Landmark Attraction (7.7km), Dimbola Lodge tearoom (13.3km)
Public transport	Bus routes 7 and 12
Parking	Moa Place long-stay car park, School Green Road
Early finish	Colwell (2km, bus route 7), Dimbola Lodge (13.3km, bus route 12 and seasonal Needles Breezer). Bus route 7 is always within walking distance until Alum Bay.

This walk, together with Walk 14 around the eastern part of Freshwater, offers a thorough exploration of 'Tennyson Country'. Broadly defined, Freshwater is an amalgamation of the small districts west of the Western Yar, and this walk explores several of them – such as Colwell, Totland, Freshwater Bay and the lovely hamlet of Middleton. A small part of the walk follows the Coastal Path, but mostly it is independent, and visits little-known gems such as Golden Hill Country Park, Freshwater Bay Church and the Farringford estate.

Facing the Vine Inn at **Freshwater** (limited accommodation, supermarkets, pub, café, restaurants, shops, toilets) turn right and almost immediately bear left into Longhalves. Abruptly turn left in 200 metres on a similar concrete path. Continue over the road, bear right, and in 200 metres go right to enter tranquil **Golden Hill Country Park**. At the far side turn left up a broad ascending track. Take a broad track right after 200 metres, with views towards Freshwater Old Village, the Western Yar and the sea to the south. Then take the parallel grassy

Freshwater Bay and Back of the Wight

path after the second bend, rejoining the track at the top. Turn left to pass the entrance to **Golden Hill Fort** (150 metres).

> The **fort** was built as one of several Palmerston Forts to protect the Solent from French incursions, but has now found a new lease of life as an unusual conglomerate of luxury houses.

From the fort, continue ahead on footpath F14 through woodland. Bear right at a path crossroads (350 metres) to reach a road in **Colwell**. Turn left, pass a bus stop, and shortly turn right into Silcombe Lane. Continue into Colwell Lane, and at the next junction go half-right (T29/F11). Cross a road past a pub to continue on Colwell Chine Road, emerging at the sandy-shingly beach of **Colwell Bay** (bar, cafés, shops, toilets): a good swimming spot. Turn left to walk along the promenade to the privately owned pier at **Totland Bay**; built in 1879 primarily to host pleasure steamers, it is currently scheduled for restoration after years of neglect.

Hath

THE
NEEDLES Old Batt
Scratchell
Ba

Continue until you reach a solitary brick building, and climb the adjacent steps. Turn right on reaching a road, and after 250 metres bear right on a signposted footpath. Emerging in the open after 500 metres, ignore a right fork to ascend **Headon Warren**. On reaching an information board (150 metres), break off from the Coastal Path by walking up the steep pathless hill on the left. Shortly bear right through a gap in the gorse bushes, and ascend to and cross the ridge, beside a signpost. Turn right immediately – parallel to the road below – and keep on this mainly level path, soon enjoying a commanding view over to the Needles.

Keep ignoring ways off the main path, including a left turn by a Coastal Path marker, staying near to or at the top of the ridge and eventually descending with the path

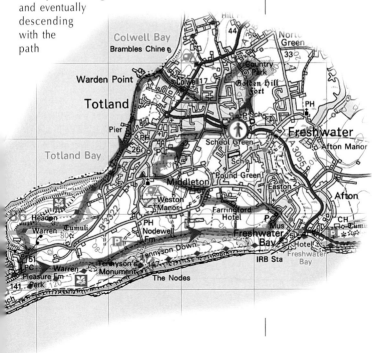

on the far side of the down. Take either path at a fork, as any descending path will eventually lead down to a drive. Turn left along the drive, and at a junction turn right to reach the entrance to **The Needles Landmark Attraction** above **Alum Bay** (bar, cafés, restaurant, shops, toilets, cable car). ◄

Time and energy permitting, you might want to descend to the bay itself by chair lift (seasonal) or footpath.

Ascend the road to pass the car park, and turn left up steps at the first corner. Continue away from the sea on a level grassy path, ignoring ways off, which soon starts to climb gradually. After crossing a gate in 1.3km you could detour up to the **Tennyson Monument** on the hill to your right (see Walk 4). To continue, stick to the gradually descending track, soon with a view of the island's Fort Albert and the mainland's Hurst Castle.

Meet a track after 700 metres and continue on a path initially between bushes. Keep to the main path, and in 950 metres ignore a left fork into trees. Coming into open downland (750 metres), strike out over the pathless grass without changing direction, shortly with a wonderful view over to Freshwater Bay and the Back of the Wight. Round a large stone house almost level with Victorian Fort Redoubt (see Walk 4) (seaward) to reach a road next to **Dimbola Lodge**.

> Victorian photographer Julia Margaret Cameron set up home at **Dimbola Lodge** after being inspired by a visit to her friend Tennyson at neighbouring Farringford. The house now hosts a permanent exhibition of her work as well as temporary exhibitions. Contemporary poet Henry Taylor remarked it was 'a house indeed to which everyone resorted for pleasure, and in which no man, woman or child was ever known to be unwelcome'. Much like today.

Turn left, past bus stops, to reach Freshwater Bay Church.

> **St Agnes Church** is the only thatched church on the island and is surprisingly modern (1908; the roof was rethatched in 1962). It was built for the benefit

Towards the thatched church, Freshwater Bay

of Freshwater Bay residents and to ease overcrowding at All Saints at the other end of the parish. The Tennysons donated the site.

A short way past the church turn left (F47). Ignore a fork on the left after 400 metres to continue under the charming wooden – but sadly disused – Tennyson's Bridge, the poet's private link to the countryside. Patrons of the accommodation and restaurant now occupying **Farringford** are welcome to enter the grounds via the 'secret' green door. Tennyson himself used the door to visit his friend and neighbour Julia Cameron in Dimbola Lodge.

Farringford was Tennyson's home from 1856 to 1867, and was host to several famous guests, such as Darwin, Garibaldi and Lewis Carroll. However, the grounds were regularly besieged by admirers, causing the despairing poet to move back to the mainland – although he did return periodically. There is self-catering accommodation and a café in the grounds, and the house is currently undergoing restoration for use as a study and cultural centre.

Witches Copse

When the track swings right, take F44 ahead. Having descended to a road, turn right through the pretty hamlet of **Middleton**, passing a couple of exquisite houses, and in 200 metres turn left (T7). By Stonewind Farm take the footpath ahead towards, and through, Witches Copse.

Turn left onto a lane and in 50 metres go right (T10). On entering a second field turn right along its edge, but do pause to admire the view over the rooftops of Totland towards the mainland beyond. Skirt clockwise round the next field and exit through a gap in the second corner. Turn left on the path ahead, and in 350 metres turn right at a path crossroads. On reaching a lane turn left, then right into Clayton Road. At its end turn left to return to the Vine Inn in **Freshwater**.

WALK 16

Shalfleet and Newtown circular

Start/Finish	New Inn, Shalfleet
Distance	11.4km (7.1 miles)
Grade	Easy
Time	3hr
Refreshments	None en route
Public transport	Bus route 7
Parking	Free car park in Mill Road, Shalfleet
Early finish	You are always within walking distance of the main road (bus route 7)

While many places on the island offer peace, quiet and dreamy vistas, certain spots such as Niton Undercliff, on the south coast, and Newtown Harbour Nature Reserve, which is explored on this walk, have their own additional charm. The harbour is just beautiful, and perhaps the best time to visit is on a sunny, windless winter's day, when you may well have the whole harbour to yourself and hear nothing but birds. Also visited on this walk are the woodland to the east (unusually bordering the saltmarsh of the nature reserve), and Newtown itself. Centuries ago Newtown was one of the island's principal towns, and many of its grassy paths were streets back then. The National Trust is prominent in Newtown, managing the nature reserve, woods, meadows and Old Town Hall.

From the New Inn at **Shalfleet** (pub, village shop), walk down Mill Road past the car park and fork left on a track shortly afterwards. Soon, parallel grassy paths offer a nicer alternative to the stony track and you find yourself walking beside Shalfleet Lake (actually a tidal creek). On reaching Shalfleet Quay do stop and savour the tranquillity of this beautiful spot – it's hard to believe that Newtown Harbour was once a bustling port. Return on the track, looking out for a gate on the right leading into a series of remote fields, carefully managed to balance the needs of

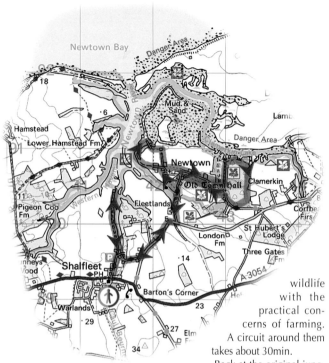

wildlife with the practical concerns of farming. A circuit around them takes about 30min.

Back at the original junction, take the other fork this time to continue down Mill Road and cross the Caul Bourne stream at the point where it feeds into Shalfleet Lake. On reaching a road turn left, but after 250 metres take a permissive path in the adjacent field. When you are led back onto the road, turn left up Town Lane and immediately after crossing a bridge over Causeway Lake (another tidal creek) turn left on footpath CB16a, initially beside the water.

The path eventually ascends to a lane by the church in **Newtown**, a graceful but relatively modern (19th century) structure built on the site of a medieval chapel. Turn left along the lane, and when it ends – with remarkable dwellings on either side – continue on CB9 to enter Coastguard Meadows.

The former pub in Newtown

Newtown was originally known as Francheville (Freetown) because of its freedom from patronage by the Lord of the Manor. The town was once the island's biggest settlement as well as one of its most prosperous, making its money exporting salt and oysters. However, a calamitous French raid in 1377 and the silting up of the harbour reversed the town's fortunes, and Newport soon overtook it in importance.

The town was awarded two parliamentary seats in 1584, but politics didn't keep up with social change, and the dwindling population soon resulted in the town becoming a 'rotten borough' (a constituency with a particularly small electorate) until the Great Reform Act of 1832 disenfranchised it. Both John Churchill, first Duke of Marlborough, and Prime Minister George Canning served the constituency which, looking at the 'town' now, seems quite astonishing.

Keeping a hedge on your left, walk round two sides of the meadow to start exploring Newtown Harbour; look for where **Newtown River** – the estuary of Shalfleet and Causeway Lakes and several other watercourses – flows into the Solent. Go through the corner gate and continue on a causeway. The serenity here, with the birdlife and bobbing boats, is wonderful.

> **Newtown Harbour (National Nature Reserve)** is a very special place indeed. It stands at the mouth of several streams, and centuries ago it was the island's principal landing area (before silting led to its decline). Today it is a profoundly peaceful and potentially therapeutic place, the very antithesis of chaotic modern life. Winter is a particularly rewarding time to visit for the experience of seeing and hearing the migrating birdlife, such as Brent geese, teal and widgeon, although a wide variety of birdlife is resident at the harbour year-round.

With a grassy path ahead, swing left with the stony causeway; at the next path junction it is possible to detour left on another causeway (muddy and uneven) to near the harbour mouth before returning. Head south, shortly crossing a long wooden bridge, and at the end of this turn left. At a bird hide, continue back to the village lane and turn left into a narrow meadow. On reaching another lane turn left, and in 650 metres, with a right bend visible ahead, find a footpath on the left to enter Town Copse.

In 400 metres, just before the woodland path leads back out into the harbour nature reserve, turn right on a path to remain just inside the wood. Keep to the current direction, the path occasionally straying back out into the nature reserve, until after about 650 metres you are led right to return deeper into the wood. At an obvious fork after 350 metres, bear right on the wider path and right again at another fork in 80 metres. Turn left at a T-junction with a grassy path and ignore path offshoots to emerge on a lane by a Walter's Copse information board.

Turn right, and in 200 metres left on CB13a to walk through a series of meadows (keeping to the current direction throughout and following any Coastal Path

Shalfleet Church

signs) to emerge on a lane where you turn left to pass the former town pub and **Newtown Old Town Hall** (see Walk 7). Descend towards the bridge over Causeway Lake (passed earlier) and continue to a T-junction. The main route from here is to return to Shalfleet the way you came: take the permissive path on the right and continue on the road when it ends, soon taking a track on your right and following it to **Shalfleet**. An alternative finish for bus travellers preferring a linear walk is to continue on CB22 opposite. In 300 metres branch left off the main track (in effect straight on) to eventually reach the main road. Turn left for the bus stops.

WALK 17
Shalfleet to Newport

Start	New Inn, Shalfleet
Finish	Newport bus station
Distance	22.2km (13.9 miles)
Grade	Fairly easy
Time	5½hr
Refreshments	Calbourne (6km)
Public transport	From start: bus route 7; from finish: bus routes 1, 2, 3, 5, 6, 7, 8, 9 and 12
Parking	Free car park in Mill Road, Shalfleet
Early finish	Newbridge (2.2km), Calbourne (6km), Newport–Yarmouth road (A3054) (10.7km), all bus route 7

This walk starts by taking in three of West Wight's 'stalwart' villages: Shalfleet, Newbridge and notably Calbourne, with its picturesque Winkle Street and water mill. Linking them is gentle, pretty countryside, where other walkers are likely to be few and far between. The real highlight however is magnificent Parkhurst Forest; surprisingly large and very beautiful, with a wide variety of tree life and vistas, it remains rather curiously an undiscovered treasure.

Before you set off it is worth visiting the church, which has an early Norman tower and several interesting features.

◄ In **Shalfleet** (pub, village shop), walk down Church Lane opposite the New Inn, and in 100 metres turn left on grassy footpath S17. Soon the Caul Bourne stream appears on the left: an occasional companion en route to Calbourne. Entering the last in a series of fields (750 metres), the path ascends half-right and leads onto a track; merge with a track coming in from the right to continue ahead, with a partial view towards Brighstone Forest. On a left bend (300 metres), bear right on S35 to arrive at a road on the edge of **Newbridge**. The village, although quaint and graceful, doesn't particularly warrant a detour. Take Clay Lane nearly opposite, beside two pretty thatched cottages.

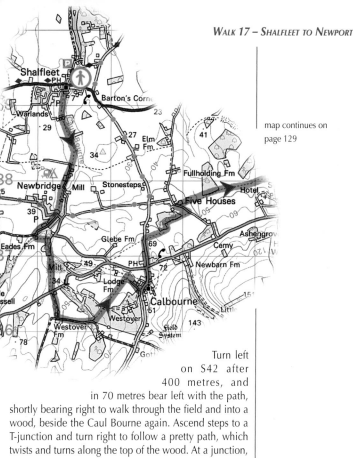

map continues on
page 129

Turn left
on S42 after
400 metres, and
in 70 metres bear left with the path,
shortly bearing right to walk through the field and into a
wood, beside the Caul Bourne again. Ascend steps to a
T-junction and turn right to follow a pretty path, which
twists and turns along the top of the wood. At a junction,
shortly after crossing the stream for the second time, it
is possible to visit Calbourne Water Mill by forking left
over a footbridge and continuing over the grass (a 10min
return detour).

Calbourne Water Mill is mentioned in the
Domesday Book and is one of the oldest working
water mills in the country. Numerous peacocks
add colour. Admission fee payable (see www.
calbournewatermill.co.uk).

Winkle Street, Calbourne

Back at the junction take the other fork to continue. Cross a road to follow the track opposite beside an unusual thatched bungalow. Merge with a track coming in from the right and turn left at a T-junction at **Westover Farm**. On an ascent after 450 metres, look out for and follow a hidden path on the left. Once out of the wood continue towards the left of the copse ahead and cross a stile, heading in the direction of now-visible Calbourne. In 500 metres, having crossed the Caul Bourne yet again, turn immediately right over the pathless grass to follow the babbling brook to and through Winkle Street, a row of lovely 18th-century cottages (some thatched) in a very photogenic setting. The street, originally called Barrington Row, has been attracting clued-up tourists for several decades.

Go left at the road ahead to walk through **Calbourne** (pub) – a village in existence at least since the ninth century – passing the 13th-century church and old village pump. Continue ahead at the Sun Inn, and after 400 metres ascend unmarked steps on the right which lead to a narrow footpath between tall hedgerows. After 350 metres walk through a vast field following the yellow arrow, soon aiming for the (as yet unseen) far left corner and turning left on a lane. In 200 metres take CB25 sharp right. Keep to the left of the field – ignore a side-field on the left – and cross to another field at the far side. Walk clockwise around it and through the first gap in the hedgerow on the far side. Bear slightly right through the next field, aiming for the hedge gap in the centre of the far side. Once through, keep to the left of the new field, from where you can see Swainston Manor, now a hotel.

> The present imposing, sumptuous building of **Swainston Manor** dates mainly from the 18th century, but a medieval chapel and hall bear testament to its days as a palace of the Bishops of Winchester, built on the site of a previous manor house dating from 735. Its name results from visits by Sweyne, Danish King of England and father of King Canute. Tennyson was a frequent visitor and paid tribute to the place in his poem 'In the Garden at Swainston'.

At a junction with a track go left, soon ignoring a right turn to keep ahead through the aesthetically pleasing Harelane Plantation. Cross a bridge over the dismantled Newport–Freshwater train line to continue to the Newport–Yarmouth road (A3054) beside bus stops. Cross the road to continue on CB26; on reaching **Three Gates Farm** bear right, and in 550 metres bear left into a wood. Emerge on a road and turn right. In 150 metres turn left on 'hidden' footpath CB8, and on entering a second field stay near the right edge. Cross a stile in the far corner to pick up CB7. Then, just after going over a stile, turn immediately left and cross a lane to continue between two back gardens (CB6). Cross a stream, walk

map continues on page 130

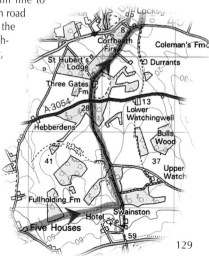

129

Harelane Plantation

right then sharp left across a field to cross a stile in its far corner. Continue past a farm to the road ahead, now in the hamlet of **Porchfield**.

Turn right, and just before the Bunts Hill road sign bear right on a grassy path. Ascend the field to the far right corner, then keep a hedgerow on your right and eventually reach a road. Turn left here, keeping eyes and ears tuned for traffic. Just after a road comes in from the left, turn right on CB5. **Parkhurst Forest** now looms ahead and walkers are soon guided into it – very much a back entrance!

Parkhurst Forest is one of the old-est forests in the country according to its owners, the Forestry Commission. It is second in size to Brighstone Forest, but significantly more imposing to walk through. King James I hunted here, and locals grazed flocks before the forest was enclosed at the start of the 19th century and com-munal rights were curtailed. Much oak planting took place subsequently to replace trees used for Nelson's navy and on former grazing land. Since 1900, periodic coniferous replanting has encouraged the island's red squirrel population, although the aim now is to increase native species while ensuring the squirrels are not driven out.

Follow the directions below carefully to avoid losing your way in the forest. Stay on the main track just after the footbridge to maintain the current direction. In 500 metres look out for an archway, and turn right through it to penetrate deeper into the forest. Go left at a T-junction in 400 metres, and, in 150 metres, where the main track swings left, bear right back into the woodland. At a T-junction (800 metres) go left, then almost immediately turn right at another one. In 70 metres turn left on a grassy path and, in 300 metres, at a junction beside a bench, go right. Ignore ways off until, after 300 metres, a crossroads with a bench on the left is reached. Turn right here and left at the next crossroads (250 metres) to reach privately owned **Signal House**, the highest point in the forest.

Bear right to walk around the house and remain on the concrete. Ignore all ways off and turn left at the T-junction by the car park. Where the drive swings right continue on the inviting path ahead, at the end of which turn right to reach the main road. Cross and turn left. By an attractive old house (250 metres) turn right on N47, and on entering a field bear half-left on a faint path in the direction of Newport Minster.

Bear half-right through a second field, and at a third keep to the right-hand edge; where the edge swings right, descend to a footbridge in the far right corner. Emerge onto a pleasant estate road and turn left both here and at the T-junction. Almost immediately turn right (N47) and bear left ahead to resume the path. Turn left at the first opportunity, left again, and then right down Mill Street. Ignore Crocker Street, but turn left into Lugley Street and take the footpath (Post Office Lane) opposite a car park. Continue up Castlehold Lane, and turn left and then right on St James' Street to arrive at the bus station in **Newport** (accommodation, supermarkets, pubs, cafés, restaurants, shops, toilets).

WALK 18

Gatcombe to Newport

Start	Gatcombe (turn-off for Gatcombe Church)
Finish	Newport bus station
Distance	10.4km (6.5 miles)
Grade	Moderate
Time	3hr
Refreshments	None en route
Public transport	To start: bus route 6 (ask the driver for the Gatcombe Church turn-off); from finish: bus routes 1, 2, 3, 5, 6, 7, 8, 9 and 12
Parking	The lane just beyond Gatcombe Church
Early finish	Carisbrooke Castle (8.2km, bus route 6)

Church aficionados will not be disappointed with the impressive one at Gatcombe at the start, and when the trees are not in leaf you may catch a glimpse of the nearby manor house from the churchyard. The route soon heads west up onto remote Garstons Down, where there is a lovely balcony path with comprehensive views; then a brook-side, but potentially boggy, path meandering towards the foot of Carisbrooke Castle. The route continues along two of the castle's outer walls, and the subsequent link path to Newport provides wonderful views over the town before the descent into its centre.

At the junction with the Newport–Chale road, take Gatcombe Road, and continue along it to **St Olave's Church**. ▶

> **St Olave's Church** at Gatcombe is a Grade I listed building built by the Estur family in the 13th century as an adjacent chapel for their property Gatcombe House (rebuilt in 1750 as a residence for the Worsley family). The church has undergone several repairs and alterations over the centuries, but

It may be possible to glimpse the facade of the splendid 18th-century Gatcombe House from the end of the churchyard path.

the font is original and the tower 15th century. It also has the only surviving example on the island of medieval stained glass in a church (in the window east of the porch). The interior hosts reclining sculptures of two past owners of Gatcombe House: Sir

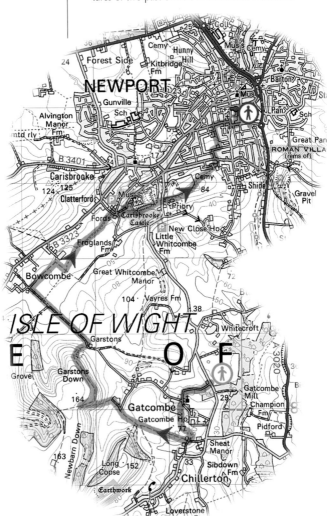

Charles Seely in the nave (who was killed in action in the First World War) and (allegedly) Edward Estur to the side of the altar, whose memorial is centuries older.

Back on the lane, turn left on an initially uphill path through woodland, and at a junction of paths just past cottages (700 metres) turn right and immediately right again onto a bridleway, soon with magisterial Tolt Copse visible ahead.

Ignore two left forks 700 metres and 800 metres from the junction, and instead descend to reach a lane. Ascend to maintain the prevalent direction, bearing left before the entrance to Newbarn Farm. On entering a field turn left, shortly taking either of the parallel paths ahead. Continue ascending **Garstons Down**, soon with a distant sea view opening up behind. At a signpost 250 metres after the parallel paths rejoin, turn right (bridleway G22). Shortly bear right again on a balcony path – it is not a widely known path but it provides a lovely stretch of walking. This is approximately the centre of the island, and the view potentially extends to East Cowes, the

A house called Garstons

Newport–Culver downland ridge, the southeast downs and the Spinnaker Tower at Portsmouth, not to mention Carisbrooke and its castle.

Eventually the path swings right and descends to proud, solitary **Garstons Farm**. Bear slightly left to take G7 signposted towards Bowcombe (keep the farm on your right initially), and just before **Bowcombe Farm** turn right on N102. Turn right at a T-junction, then in 150 metres go left on N104 and continue with marshy Lukely Brook on the left, which flows into the Medina further along its course. ◄ Maintain this direction, ignoring all ways off. Eventually cross a pretty stream and emerge onto a lane. Although you may not see it, you are just below **Carisbrooke Castle**. Turn right on this lane, then at the junction with Millers Lane continue on N88, signposted to the castle. On reaching the car park, turn left to leave it and immediately take the path beside the outer castle walls (or to visit the castle walk down the road for a minute to the entrance).

If the path is too swampy here, consult the map for alternatives along a parallel road or other footpaths.

The foundations of the present **Carisbrooke Castle** were built on the site of a Roman fort by the first Lord of the Island and friend of William the Conqueror, one William FitzOsbern, shortly after

Carisbrooke Castle

the Norman invasion. Fortified by his nephew Richard de Redvers, the castle served both as an important primary defence against foreign invaders and as the official residence of the island's Lords and, subsequently, Governors. It fulfilled this function until the last resident Governor Princess Beatrice's death in 1944. The castle's national claim to fame is as the site of Charles I's imprisonment for over a year before his beheading in 1649. Maintained today by English Heritage, the castle is one of the island's premier visitor attractions and is well worth a visit. Look out for the resident donkeys which for centuries have drawn water from its well.

On reaching the start of the castle's third side, immediately take the path between two wooden gates, shortly crossing a road beside bus stops and taking the steps opposite (N25). Beyond the steps the path rises gradually, soon with marvellous, ever-expanding views beside Carisbrooke Cemetery.

The path descends to a suburban road; go left and take the first right (Elm Grove). Start walking anti-clockwise around the playing field ahead – an attractive setting even this close to the centre of Newport. By a metal post, descend the adjacent concrete path, ignore South View soon on the left and, at the T-junction beyond, turn right to reach another T-junction. Go right again past a former school (built 1904), take the first left into Medina Avenue, then turn left again to walk through Church Litten Park.

Church Litten Park was once a burial ground, founded in 1582 to house plague victims, but was turned into a park by the first female mayor of Newport in 1931. Look out for the magnificent Weeping Beech tree – its melancholic quality a reminder of the park's former use.

The bus station at **Newport** (accommodation, supermarkets, pubs, cafés, restaurants, shops, toilets) is at the end of the park.

WALK 19
Tennyson Trail

Start	Carisbrooke Church
Finish	Freshwater Bay
Distance	17.3km (10.8 miles)
Grade	Fairly easy, with one steep stretch near the end
Time	4hr
Refreshments	None en route
Public transport	To start: bus routes 7 and 12; from finish: bus route 12 or the seasonal Needles Breezer to Yarmouth for a connection with bus route 7
Parking	Short-stay car park in Carisbrooke High Street; alternatively, try Priory Road
Early finish	No easy options

The popular, easy-to-follow Tennyson Trail is a fantastic way of getting to the stunning Back of the Wight from Newport's neighbour, Carisbrooke. It generally keeps to ridges throughout its entire length and can be divided into three distinct parts: Bowcombe Down, Brighstone Forest, and the downland overlooking the southwest coastline. The last runs parallel to the Coastal Path way down below and heads across a landscape of ever increasing beauty and drama. The trail is satisfyingly remote and encounters few man-made structures – at least until the hilltop golf course near the end. This walk ends at Freshwater Bay, which is arguably the perfect place to stop; those who have the energy to continue via the Needles to the trail's official end at Alum Bay should refer to Walk 4.

At the crossroads just up from the church in **Carisbrooke** (supermarket, pubs, restaurants, shops, toilets), ascend Carisbrooke High Street, and in 200 metres bear left on Nodgham Lane. After 100 metres bear right uphill: the official start of the trail. Ascend gradually to where the path levels out just below the top of **Bowcombe Down**; the route stays at this lofty height for most of the walk.

Views appear and disappear, both easterly (look out for Carisbrooke Castle) and later northwesterly towards the mainland. ▶

When you have the first view of the Solent (2.5km from the start of the trail), bear left. At a

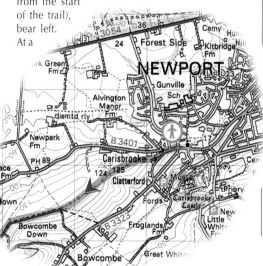

Five Barrows

If you're inspired to write poetry up here you wouldn't be alone: apparently this is where John Keats wrote the famous line from Endymion: 'A thing of beauty is a joy for ever'.

map continues on page 141

139

map continues on
page 142

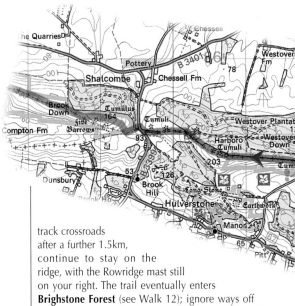

track crossroads
after a further 1.5km,
continue to stay on the
ridge, with the Rowridge mast still
on your right. The trail eventually enters
Brighstone Forest (see Walk 12); ignore ways off
the main track until a T-junction after a further 1.7km.
Turn right, now with a wonderful view of the Back of the
Wight coastline and sharing your way with the Worsley
Trail.

Eventually reach a road; cross it to the right and continue, to start ascending Mottistone Down. Ignore a right
fork beyond the car park and in a further 1.4km the path
levels out beside a gate; notice the 4000-year-old barrows (burial mounds) on the right.

The downs of the Back of the Wight were an **ancient
trading route** as the shore was too inhospitable and
other areas less navigable. That the Neolithic peo-
ples chose to bury their dead on the route itself was
a mark of respect.

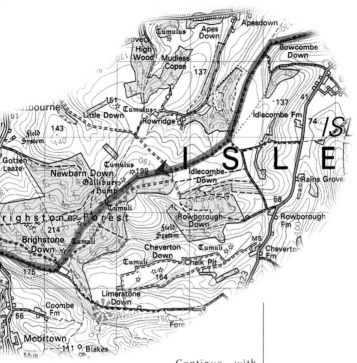

Continue, with an incredible two-coast panorama shortly unfolding. While descending, spot the 'white line' snaking up the hill ahead; this is your onward trail, but thankfully it's not quite as steep as it looks! On reaching a road, continue along the track opposite, up Brook Down, shortly bearing right with the chalk track. When you feel ready, bear half-right off the track to climb the grassy escarpment, very steeply, heading towards the top of the down. The top is known as **Five Barrows**, although there are actually eight. The panoramic view is sensational.

Continue in the direction of the chalk cliffs of High Down, eventually rejoining the track left earlier, now on a splendid ridge. Enter a golf course about 1.7km from Five Barrows, the northerly view opening up again. In 1.5km bear left on a trail-signposted footpath. On reaching the

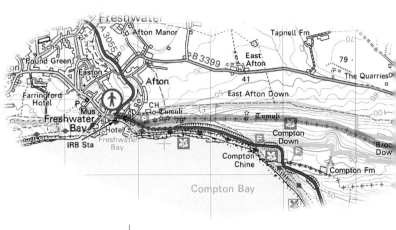

Approaching Freshwater Bay

coastal road turn right along it to descend to **Freshwater Bay** (limited accommodation, hotel bar, cafés, shop, toilets); bus stops are just beyond the Albion Hotel.

EAST WIGHT

St Catherine's Oratory Lighthouse (Walks 11 and 24)

WALK 20
Shanklin circular via Nettlecombe

Start/Finish	High Street, Shanklin Old Village
Distance	27.6km (17.3 miles)
Grade	Moderate
Time	7hr
Refreshments	Shop at the donkey sanctuary (6.9km). Although this long and occasionally demanding walk offers almost no opportunities for refreshments, there are several places to picnic and several opportunities to cut the walk short.
Public transport	Bus routes 2 and 3, and train
Parking	Orchardleigh Road long-stay car park (off High Street)
Early finish	Whiteley Bank (6.6km, bus route 3), Dean Farm (14.7km, bus route 6), near Ventnor (17.8km, bus route 6), several opportunities from Ventnor Cemetery to just beyond Luccombe Farm (20.7km–25.0km, bus route 3)

This walk provides a perfect introduction to the beautiful downland and coastal scenery of the island's southeast corner. There are lovely views throughout, which constantly change, and indeed the top of St Martin's Down and the Worsley Monument are arguably the two best viewpoints on the island. The walk initially explores the downs on either side of the Wroxall valley, connected by a donkey sanctuary in the valley itself. Further west is the isolated and evocative hamlet of Nettlecombe, followed by an 'alternative Coastal Path' – more dramatic than the official path – high above St Lawrence, Ventnor and finally Bonchurch before descending to the gorgeous hamlet of Luccombe, which the Coastal Path only bypasses.

Descend High Street through the Old Village in **Shanklin** (accommodation, supermarkets, pubs, cafés, restaurants, shops, toilets) and turn left beside Pencil Cottage to pass the top entrance to **Shanklin Chine** (see Walk 1). Ignore the steps on the left to continue up to a junction, turning right onto Popham Road. At the T-junction take Vaughan

Shanklin Old Village

Way almost opposite; branch right on a footpath in 100 metres, soon emerging opposite Shanklin Old Church. Turn left, and in 400 metres left on SS8. Take the faint path ahead, and when it peters out bear quarter-right across the field.

Look out for, and cross, a stile in the treeline opposite (located some 150 metres from the gate in the corner of the field), shortly re-emerging on the main road. Turn left and, opposite a bus stop, go sharp right on SS9a, soon bearing left to gradually ascend the slopes of **Shanklin Down**. On eventually reaching the top, ignore the initial forks and turn right at the T-junction just beyond (V40), soon walking on a broad grassy path.

Keep to the main path along the ridge and as it bears left in 650 metres. After a further 450 metres ignore a path offshoot right, and just beyond the approaching hedgerow ascend half-left over pathless grass, shortly to reach the top of **St Martin's Down** and a sweeping panoramic view. Freemantle Gate and the Worsley Monument

145

(passed later) are visible to the north of Appuldurcombe House (beyond Wroxall).

Retrace your steps to take the aforementioned path offshoot sharp left. Go through a gate to enter woodland (450 metres) and keep to the main descending path. At a path crossroads in 250 metres turn left (V34). Ignore ways off until the track is blocked (400 metres); turn right here onto V49, and 200 metres later turn left through a gate to continue on a faint grassy path through two fields in the direction of Godshill, again enjoying a near-panoramic view.

Donkey sanctuary

The sanctuary was established in 1987 to provide any donkey in distress, or otherwise in need of care and attention, with a safe and permanent home.

Descend half-right through a third field (no path initially) to exit in the far corner. Cross the dismantled Shanklin–Ventnor railway line to continue down to a road just south of the hamlet of **Whiteley Bank** beside bus stops. Cross to your right to follow NC43, which runs through a very charming **donkey sanctuary**. ◄

Eventually cross a lane and ascend the footpath opposite. Pass Freemantle Gate on the left (450 metres) to carry straight on (GL49).

Freemantle Gate is a very evocative and photogenic 18th-century neoclassical folly, built as an imposing entrance to the Worsley family's Appuldurcombe Estate.

In a further 450 metres turn abruptly left (GL63) to climb very steeply up the grassy slope. About 70 metres beyond a mini-plateau of sorts bear left, shortly skirting clockwise around a hollow towards the **Worsley Monument** on the hill ahead. The view once you get there is possibly the most comprehensive on the island: the Back of the Wight, High Down, Carisbrooke Castle, the Solent, Culver/Bembridge Down and the suburbs of Ventnor are all visible on a clear day.

> The **Worsley Monument** was erected in 1774 in memory of Sir Robert Worsley by his grandson Sir Richard (the hill was part of the Worsleys' Appuldurcombe Estate). In 1831 a lightning strike shortened it from its original height of 21m (70ft).

Head south towards a transmitter, with Wroxall down on the left (there will shortly be a faint path, staying more-or-less on the ridge). At a path T-junction turn left onto GL58. On reaching the start of a track take GL51 sharp right. Just beyond the gate ahead turn right along the field edge, in 350 metres crossing another (metal) gate and a wooden gate in a further 300 metres; then in 80 metres turn left down a footpath in woodland. Pass farm buildings on your right after 450 metres, and in a further 150 metres follow a yellow arrow left over a stile and bear half-right towards a stile soon visible in the hedgerow on the far side of the field (stay clear of the copse to the left).

Head half-left through a second field (in the direction of St Catherine's Down) to the corner of another copse, then continue with the copse on your left. Cross into a third field and bear half-right to exit it, turning left on the track. In 100 metres turn right over a footbridge, and at a path junction carry straight on (GL54a). In 350 metres turn left over a footbridge and stiles and immediately right to go through a gate, soon reaching a lane. Keep ahead through the hamlet of **Nettlecombe**, and turn right beyond Nettlecombe Farm (NT5) to pass three fishing lakes.

> The hamlet of **Nettlecombe** was the site of a larger village in medieval times, as evidenced by nearby earthworks. Perhaps one day they will be excavated and more will be learnt about the village that was. A likely reason for the decline of the village was the nationwide shift from a labour-intensive and community-focused arable economy to a more dispersed pastoral one.

At a junction with a track near the village of **Whitwell** turn left (NT12). Shortly turn right over a stile beyond houses and continue through the centre of an oblong-shaped field and a second field to reach a road at **Dean Farm**, opposite the bus stop for Newport. Turn right, and after 100 metres go left down St Rhadagund's Path. ◀

The Ventnor bus stop is obscured by bushes just beyond the junction.

> The start of the path runs parallel to the course of the former **Merstone–Ventnor West railway line** on the right, before the latter disappears under a tunnel. When running, it was described as one of the prettiest branch lines in England.

Cross a stile in 650 metres to continue over the grass towards the 'High Hat' crossroads, which Coastal Path walkers will be familiar with (see Walk 2). But whereas the route of the Coastal Path to Shanklin descends from here to St Lawrence and stays on the low sea cliffs, and Undercliff beyond Ventnor, the onward route maintains significantly higher ground while not forsaking the fantastic sea views. So turn left on this stunning balcony path overlooking **St Lawrence**. In 650 metres – shortly after the path heads inland – branch right down steps to a lane and ascend the other side. Turn right at the top,

View over St Lawrence

shortly continuing on another balcony path (although this time the view is somewhat obstructed by a hedgerow). In 300 metres ignore a right fork into the trees. The path shortly runs parallel to a road and eventually passes more bus stops. Shortly after, the footpath finally emerges onto the road, but in 80 metres look out for and ascend V64, and in a further 70 metres take an unmarked path left between fences to ascend **Rew Down**.

Turn left immediately past the kissing gate and in 200 metres keep to the main fork as it swings uphill to the right. Once over the stile at the top turn left and almost immediately turn right to climb further up the down between gorse bushes. On coming out onto a golf course, take the footpath to the left, and at a T-junction turn right; in 200 metres turn right again on a signposted footpath to walk through the **golf course**. Keep more or less to the ridge, initially gradually ascending, and with spectacular views both south and north.

Pass to the left of the clubhouse, and at the far end of the course pass the 11th tee, with a sensational view towards Ventnor. Start to descend the down, and almost immediately after a bend to the right, turn left into trees. Cross a gap in the stone wall to enter **Ventnor Cemetery** and turn right to walk around its perimeter, soon continuing on concrete. Beside a stone lodge find and descend steps to a road. ▸

From here to Luccombe Farm the walk is never far from bus route 3, which runs along the main road at the foot of the downs.

Take Old Shute opposite and resist the tempting path leading into Old Shute Field some way along. Instead emerge on a walkway above the main road and follow it left, soon passing Ventnor Industrial Estate.

This used to be **Ventnor Station**, the terminus of trains from Ryde. Walk to the far side to see a boarded-up tunnel, which is where steam trains used to emerge from deep under St Boniface Down.

After a further 350 metres turn left up V110 to continue just above the rooftops of Ventnor. In 400 metres ignore the gate ahead to bear left, staying on the edge of the wood and ascending very steeply. The path shortly levels out and penetrates deeper through this rather dark and sinister wood. Ignore descending forks, and soon ascend even higher. Having exited the wood, the path continues up a remote section of **St Boniface Down** but swings right just before the severely steep incline. Look to your right for one of the most beautiful views of the walk: the rooftops of Ventnor have now given way to those of the quieter village of Bonchurch – a vista somewhat reminiscent of the earlier hilltop views over Ventnor's other (western) neighbour, St Lawrence.

Stay on this wonderful path, just above the houses of **Bonchurch**, until it finally meets the road again opposite a car park. Turn left, and in 200 metres go right (SS6), with yet another stunning view ahead. Soon descend a long flight of steps through a tunnel of trees (the steps may be slippery and in poor condition so hold onto the rail). Down in the valley, cross a stile on the other side of a track to maintain your previous direction. Having reached Luccombe Farm, walk round the stone wall of the beautiful farmhouse and remain on the concrete drive.

At a hairpin bend, continue ahead over a stile on a grassy track. In 90 metres bear left, ignoring steps a little way along. ◄ Once at the start of the hamlet of **Luccombe** take SS88 on the right, shortly continuing on a grassy footpath. When the path ends, turn left to walk through the hamlet's main street. Maintain your current direction beyond the hamlet, bearing left opposite Haddon's Pits to continue back towards **Shanklin**. At the T-junction with Popham Road take the descending path opposite to return via the Chine to High Street.

For bus stops take these steps to ascend back to the road.

Luccombe Farm

WALK 21

Shanklin circular via Bonchurch

Start/Finish	High Street, Shanklin Old Village
Distance	10.5km (6.6 miles)
Grade	Moderate
Time	2½hr
Refreshments	Bonchurch (5.4km)
Public transport	Bus routes 2 and 3, and train (the train station is a 10min walk)
Parking	Orchardleigh Road long-stay car park (off High Street)
Early finish	Bonchurch (4.7km, bus route 3), top of Devil's Chimney (7.7km, bus route 3)

This fantastic walk explores some of the loftiest points on the Isle of Wight, on top of Shanklin, Luccombe and Bonchurch Downs. An altitude of 240m (787ft) may not sound like much, but after experiencing the views down to Bonchurch and the sea, they will doubtless stay in your memory (in mist these views can be wonderfully ethereal). Numerous steps link the three 'strata' of Bonchurch; at the lowest the walk meanders beside Bonchurch Pond and descends still further to the village's 1000-year-old church. Finally the Coastal Path is followed through The Landslip and pretty coastal fringes of Luccombe back into Shanklin.

From the short-stay car park in the Old Village High Street in **Shanklin** (accommodation, supermarkets, pubs, cafés, restaurants, shops, toilets), walk uphill for a short way and take the first left (Pomona Road). At the junction with Grange Road continue ahead and, where Westhill Road starts, continue in your current direction (footpath SS84). Go left at a T-junction to reach a duck pond on the left and Shanklin Old Church on the right. ▶

Enter the churchyard and take SS10 at the back of the church to start the ascent up **Shanklin Down**, soon with most of Sandown Bay visible behind. Eventually ascend a

The 850-year-old church was for centuries the private chapel of Shanklin Manor before being granted to the Old Village parish in Victorian times.

flight
of steps
shortly followed
by another, after which
there is a steep rise. Go through the swing gate at the top
of this rise (by a signpost), and then immediately turn left,
following the pathless field edge. Entering the next field,
bear half-right to climb to the **trig point** at the top of the
hill, where the most glorious panoramic view awaits. On
a clear day the entire width of the island from Culver Cliff
to High Down is visible.

Continuing in the same direction, shortly go over
two stiles and turn left, now with a peaceful lonely valley
on your right, and the village of Wroxall nestling within
it. Stay on this ridge-top path, soon entering Luccombe
Down. Having been on the ridge for 1.4km, and with
a gate just visible 200 metres ahead, branch left onto a

wide stony path. Ignore ways off the main path, shortly arriving at a makeshift car park. Walk towards the bench and National Trust sign on the left, and go right on the grassy path, ignoring the spur almost immediately on your left. Head towards the glistening sea and take V42 to enter Bonchurch Down. The descent is steep, but the seascape stunning.

If the path is unclear, aim for the rightmost of the cluster of houses immediately below the precise slope you are on. Steps lead down to a road through **Upper Bonchurch**, near bus stops. Cross and turn left to almost immediately descend some (initially metal) steps, which soon carve

Descending from one part of Bonchurch to another

their way through rock. Turn right at the road below, which soon becomes a footpath, and descend via more steps to the road through picturesque **Bonchurch** (limited accommodation, pub, restaurant). Turn left to pass the lovely pond (filled with carp), an upmarket restaurant and several interesting old houses. Shortly after the houses end, bear right downhill towards the 11th-century Old Church.

> **Bonchurch** is mentioned in the *Domesday Book*, and its Old Church was built in 1070. Farming, fishing and quarrying were the principal occupations of the small population for centuries, the stone being exported by sea to other island and mainland locations. The village expanded rapidly in the mid-19th century, necessitating the building of a new church. But the Old Church has the charm, especially its lovely churchyard with gravestones dating to at least the early 1600s. King Charles I visited the church, apparently, paying tribute at a friend's funeral, and Charles Dickens is known to have stayed in the village while working on *David Copperfield*.

Bonchurch Old Church

Continue descending after visiting the church; after 40 metres take a sharp left, now on the Coastal Path, the signs for which should be followed all the way back to Shanklin. Bear right after 30 metres, and opposite The Boat House go left to continue, following the coastline. Ignore all ways off the main path, eventually entering the rich broadleaved woodland of **The Landslip** (so called because of the erosion and intermittent landslides that have affected the area since the last ice age). ▶

Go through a swing gate at the end of The Landslip and continue on a wide track. At a track junction (100 metres), take the right fork, bearing right after 200 metres and staying on the main path, always keeping to the same direction. After passing several secluded, beautifully situated properties (part of the hamlet of **Luccombe**), and shortly after emerging on concrete, your goal – Shanklin – is eventually seen at the forefront of the magnificent swoop of Sandown Bay.

Continue ahead at the road junction over the rise, but shortly beyond it bear left off the road and continue adjacent to it in a field, to emerge back onto it at the far right corner. Then, at the T-junction with Popham Road, continue through Rylstone Gardens, bearing left at the sculpture. Descend steps, pass the top entrance of **Shanklin Chine** (see Walk 1) – worth visiting, if not necessarily today – and continue back up to **Shanklin Old Village**.

To cut the walk short, look out for V65c, also known as the Devil's Chimney, in the middle of The Landslip (if you don't mind climbing the 225 steps to reach the bus stops at the top).

WALK 22
Shanklin circular via America Wood

Start/Finish	Shanklin bus stands, Carter Avenue
Distance	9.5km (5.9 miles)
Grade	Moderate
Time	2½hr
Refreshments	None en route
Public transport	Bus routes 2 and 3, and train
Parking	Shanklin Station car park
Early finish	Newport–Shanklin Road (A3020) (3.1km and 8.5km, bus route 2)

This short walk offers an effective introduction to both the downland southwest of Shanklin and atmospheric America Wood. The latter half makes use of permissive paths near and through Holme Copse, planted by a former High Sheriff to form a link with Greatwood and Hungerberry copses, its two ancient neighbours. Little-used footpaths then lead up to the base of Sibden Hill and back to Batts Copse, two areas of Shanklin greenery not usually frequented by visitors. Do not tackle the latter part of this walk if fog is forecast, as careful route-finding is needed to descend from the downs.

From the bus stands at **Shanklin** (accommodation, supermarkets, pubs, cafés, restaurants, shops, toilets), turn right along Collingwood Road (opposite the café), then immediately left on footpath SS15. Cross a road and soon reach Batts Copse; keep a stream on your left, and turn right when there are steps ahead and a footbridge on the left. Cross Carter Avenue and, at a T-junction ahead, turn left; turn right shortly after to pass above what was once the Shanklin–Ventnor railway line and is now a track for walkers and cyclists.

Keep ahead at the next junction and bear left at the next. Almost immediately bear left again onto the grass to find and follow a path between large fields. At the

far side, continue in the same direction towards farm buildings, with a view of Bembridge Down now behind.

View from Shanklin Down

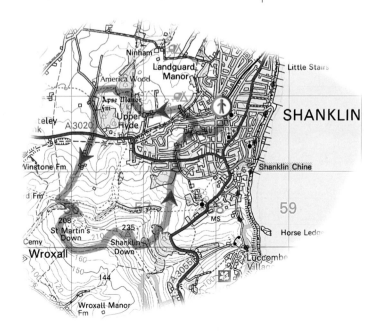

Allegedly so called because its trees were used to build ships to fight the American War of Independence, America Wood is coniferous in parts but mainly broadleaved (notably oak).

Bus stops are to the left.

Ignore ways off your current direction, and eventually descend through trees. At an isolated stone house 600 metres from the farm, turn left on a path to enter **America Wood**. ◄

Stay in your current direction, but after 150 metres take a wide path on the left (or continue on your current path to start a circuit of the wood). Turn right at a junction after 70 metres to descend and leave the wood. On reaching a lane, turn left and after 300 metres bear right on NC30a. Bear left on an enclosed path after 70 metres, which brings you to the Newport–Shanklin road (A3020). ◄ Cross and continue under a former railway line (the same line as was crossed earlier) to start the ascent of **St Martin's Down** – the northeastern stretch of the arc of downland centred on the village of Wroxall.

At a junction of paths after 1.2km go through the gate ahead and turn left just inside the wood (V46). Go through another gate (250 metres) and bear half-right continuing to gradually ascend the down, still with an outstanding view behind of Sandown Bay and the Solent. The faint path shortly becomes a track; continue along it, looking through gaps in the hedge for an uncommon view of Freemantle Gate, Wroxall, Appuldurcombe House, Stenbury Down and the Back of the Wight. Skirt round the hill on your left, ignoring ways off; then, after 850 metres on the track, bear left uphill on a wide, grassy path. Once at the saddle, turn right along the clear path. Perhaps pause at the forthcoming path junction to admire the stunning view north.

Keep ahead; in 100 metres turn left over a stile, and continue to the trig point on top of **Shanklin Down**. Start descending directly towards Shanklin on a very faint path, but just after a pit on the right (100 metres), turn right across the pathless grass towards a line of trees bordered by a fence. Aim for the furthest tree, then find and cross a stile. Descend with the wood on the left, soon swinging left on a clear path to enter it.

Cross a stile (80 metres) and continue on a very faint path towards, and into, Greatwood Copse, shortly bearing right at a junction. In 150 metres turn left on a

Holme Copse

permissive path and at a path crossroads (250 metres) continue straight on, almost immediately bearing left towards Holme Copse.

> **Holme Copse** was planted in 2003–04 by Anne Springman, former island High Sheriff and descendant of one of the first Lords of the Manor of Shanklin, active in the 12th century. The permissive paths are courtesy of her.

Facing the wood, turn right, keeping it on your left, and after 150 metres bear left, staying with the wood. In 250 metres enter and quickly exit Hungerberry Copse (which counts wild cherry among its trees), and in 40 metres turn left down steps and descend a grassy path. Take a left fork after 100 metres, which leads to a road (now back in **Shanklin**). Go left, cross Victoria Avenue (beside bus stops) and descend Chatsworth Avenue. Where the road swings right, continue ahead on SS99. Descend a minor path to the right 100 metres after entering a wood – although Sibden Hill is worth exploring first by taking one of the paths on the left – and turn right at the T-junction shortly afterwards. Eventually, descend steps to the crossroads in Batts Copse, which was passed at the start of the walk. Go straight across and follow the paths back to the bus stands.

WALK 23
Shanklin to Godshill

Start	Shanklin Station
Finish	Godshill
Distance	7.4km (4.6 miles)
Grade	Fairly easy
Time	2hr
Refreshments	None en route
Public transport	To start: train and bus route 3 (bus route 2 stops nearby); from finish: bus routes 2 and 3
Parking	Station car park
Early finish	Apse Heath (2.8km, bus route 8)

This short and easy walk makes for a pleasant two-hour ramble between Shanklin, a popular resort on the east coast, and Godshill, one of the island's idyllic honey-pot villages. Make sure to leave time to look around Godshill: stroll up to the beguiling 15th-century church, see the model village, have tea in a quaint café, and mingle with more 'mainstream' tourists (who probably won't be encountered on the walk itself, even at the lovely secluded ponds at Ninham).

Facing the station at **Shanklin** (accommodation, supermarkets, pubs, cafés, restaurants, shops, toilets) turn left and walk down the steps, turning right at the bottom. Look for, and follow, bridleway SS18 on the left, and turn right at a T-junction at a holiday home area. In 200 metres bear left through a gate, and turn left at a track T-junction (SS18a). After 400m a right turn leads to the ponds at **Ninham**, a pleasant place to picnic. Swing right after the larger pond (SS58), shortly ascending a broad track. Just after a fairly steep section, look down to the left for a comprehensive view towards America Wood.

Just before reaching the barn visible ahead, turn right on an unsigned path and left by the pumping

map opposite
continues on page 164

Pond at Ninham

station. ▶ Soon cross a road and continue on NC28, shortly alternating left and right. At the far side of a field, turn right beside a solitary house, following the yellow arrow. In 100 metres, be sure to turn left just before another house (no clear path). Cross the next road and continue (NC27), soon enjoying near-panoramic views, including Godshill on the horizon.

If you want to end the walk, continue ahead at the pumping station until the road at Apse Heath for bus stops.

Turn left at a track junction to eventually descend to an isolated pond (unlike at Ninham, there is not even a farmhouse to keep it company). Soon after crossing a plank-bridge turn left and cross the stream again (ignore a fork to the right). Bear slightly left in the field beyond, soon crossing a lane and taking the broad track opposite (GL28), with the Chillerton and

163

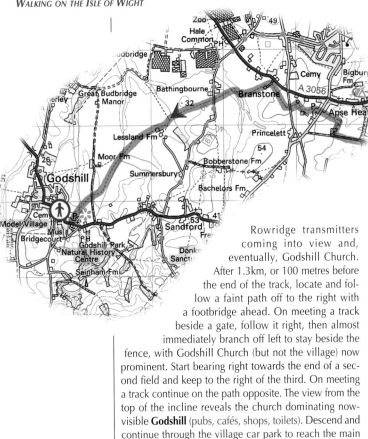

Rowridge transmitters coming into view and, eventually, Godshill Church. After 1.3km, or 100 metres before the end of the track, locate and follow a faint path off to the right with a footbridge ahead. On meeting a track beside a gate, follow it right, then almost immediately branch off left to stay beside the fence, with Godshill Church (but not the village) now prominent. Start bearing right towards the end of a second field and keep to the right of the third. On meeting a track continue on the path opposite. The view from the top of the incline reveals the church dominating now-visible **Godshill** (pubs, cafés, shops, toilets). Descend and continue through the village car park to reach the main street.

WALK 24

Niton circular (the two lighthouses walk)

Start/Finish	Niton village centre (Norris Grocers)
Distance	14.5km (9.1 miles)
Grade	Moderate
Time	4hr
Refreshments	Buddle Inn (10.1km and 13.2km)
Public transport	Bus route 6
Parking	Niton Library has a car park (Star Inn Road)
Early finish	Near Blackgang (6.5km, bus route 6), Niton (7.8km, bus route 6), outskirts of Niton (13.3km, bus route 6)

This is a fantastic walk of two contrasting halves and just as enjoyable in winter as the warmer months. The first half treads the downland above Niton, specifically the little-known Head Down and the much more popular St Catherine's Down, which hosts the Hoy Monument and 14th-century St Catherine's Oratory Lighthouse, also known as the Pepper Pot. This should not be confused with the newer St Catherine's Lighthouse on the southern tip of the island, seen in its spectacular glory from the Coastal Path. The second half of this walk descends the cliffs to the lighthouse and the secluded village of Niton Undercliff, with its almost Mediterranean feel. Choose a sunny day to capitalise on the sea views, some of which are among the best on the island.

From the grocery store at **Niton** (shops, toilets) walk along Church Street (opposite Rectory Road). Just before the church turn right into Pan Lane, and 250 metres further turn right again on footpath NT54 to walk through a farm. Once past it, ascend half-left towards a field gate on the lower slopes of **Head Down**. Keep a fence on your right in the next field – Niton is visible to the right, and the village of Whitwell and hamlet of Nettlecombe ahead. Walk round two sides of this field; midway along the second side, cross a stile onto a short, pretty path. Turn left at the

T-junction, then almost immediately right over a stile, again keeping the field edge on your right. The glorious near-panoramic view is worth savouring. Downcourt Farm, visible below St Catherine's Down, will be passed soon.

Cross a stile to steeply descend the next field. Start descending a third field, but bear half-left (off path) near the end to cross a gate beside an isolated thatched holiday cottage. March straight across the pathless grass to spot and cross a stile into a vast field. Keeping to the same direction, in about 300 metres and when nearly level with a metal gate over on the left, bear half-right to locate and cross a less conspicuous gate. Head towards the **Downcourt Farm** complex (currently let year-round as holiday accommodation), and just beyond Hermitage Court Farm turn left up a grassy bank. Immediately past a wooden gate (300 metres) turn sharp right along a lovely balcony path, enhanced by bluebells in spring and stretches of gorse.

See Walk 11 for the history of the Hoy Monument, and of St Catherine's Oratory Lighthouse (see below).

On reaching a stone wall ascend the escarpment, shortly bearing right to reach the top – detour right to reach the **Hoy Monument**. ▸ Retrace your steps briefly, but continue along the ridge. Take either fork whenever the path divides, then beyond a gate bear half-left and turn right at a fence to ascend **St Catherine's Hill** and eventually reach **St Catherine's Oratory Lighthouse**. After admiring the sensational vista, bear half-right towards the sea, shortly with a view down towards Blackgang Chine.

Beyond a gate, bear half-left towards the higher and smaller of the two car parks visible. Having descended to the point where the slope becomes significantly steeper, turn left on a faint path. ▸ Continue on the path until a concrete drive. ▸

To end the walk here by taking the bus towards Newport, continue towards the car park to find the bus stop on the other side of the road.

Turn left and immediately right (NT52), with Niton soon coming back into view. Eventually you reach the road on the edge of the village. Cross it to take NT33.

For the bus towards Ventnor, turn right to reach the road and bus stop.

Cross two stiles and go right at a T-junction, now on the Coastal Path. After 700 metres, by a bench and signpost and with a breathtaking seaward view, descend very steeply left on a magical little footpath; the foliage provides a marked contrast to the relative bareness of the clifftops.

Reach a lane at the bottom of the path – once part of a road to Blackgang before becoming a victim of erosion. Turn left, now in dreamy Niton Undercliff. Turn right at a road, and right again after 100 metres. ▸ After 500 metres continue on a gravel track into the **Knowles Farm Estate** (owned by the National Trust). Guglielmo Marconi conducted early wireless experiments behind the farmhouse in 1900, and the base of a communication mast can still be seen.

Alternatively, you may wish to detour left at the second junction to the 16th-century Buddle Inn (100 metres) (there is another opportunity to visit later).

Cottages, Niton Undercliff

Niton Undercliff is the island's most southerly village. Truly idyllic and under-explored (perhaps due to its relative inaccessibility), it developed into a proper community only in Victorian times, and it forms the western extremity of the wider Undercliff, which stretches to Ventnor. Its lush vegetation is testament to its warm microclimate, and it certainly possesses a very special ambience. Marconi stayed and worked at the Royal Sandrock Hotel (near the Buddle Inn), which sadly burned down in the 1980s.

Continue past the farm, now holiday cottages, on a 'grass carpet', and meander down to the sea. The effects of erosion are all too clear here. It is possible to detour over the stile in the corner to explore, but the onward route is to follow the coastline east on a path of sorts along the cliff edge. On reaching the perimeter wall of **St Catherine's Lighthouse** walk around its three navigable sides and continue, still following the coastline.

St Catherine's Lighthouse

Located on the island's southerly point and commissioned after the notorious *Clarendon* shipwreck in 1836, **St Catherine's Lighthouse** went into operation in 1840 to replace the defunct lighthouse on top of St Catherine's Hill, passed earlier. The new lighthouse was somewhat revolutionary in design and produced a particularly powerful light by contemporary standards (its current range is 26 nautical miles). It is open for guided tours daily in summer.

Having passed some not very private holiday homes, turn left at a concrete T-junction (or make the short detour right to rest or picnic at Castlehaven Green). Bend right with the lane, with marvellous sea views all the while. ▸

At a T-junction turn right, and at the next, take 'the tunnels' footpath opposite, and continue ahead at a junction. Turn right at the next junction (NT26), and at a five-path junction after 450 metres, continue ahead (the second path clockwise). Ignore ways off, and on reaching a road turn left to return to the grocery store at **Niton**.

For a first or second visit to the Buddle Inn, detour left up NT43 shortly after the bend.

WALK 25
Ashey Station circular

Start/Finish	Ashey Station
Alternative start/finish	Newchurch
Distance	15km (9.4 miles)
Grade	Moderate
Time	3½hr
Refreshments	Newchurch only
Public transport	Steam train to Ashey. Newchurch is accessible by the seasonal Downs Breezer from Ryde.
Parking	Newchurch car park (Ashey Station is accessible only to pedestrians)
Early finish	No alternatives besides Ashey Station and Newchurch

Ashey Station must be one of the quaintest and most pleasantly located railway stations in England and is the perfect place to start a country walk. When the steam trains are running, it is usually possible to arrive on the first train from either direction and complete the walk in time for the last departure (but note that Ashey is a request stop so make sure you tell the guard you intend to alight there). The station only has pedestrian access, so drivers are advised to start at Newchurch. But wherever you start, this is a lovely walk best done when the trees are in leaf. Highlights are Martin's Wood/Newchurch Bee Fields, Ashey Sea Mark, and some of the most delightful woodland on the island.

In 1966 the **Ryde to Cowes railway line** was one of the final victims of the dismantling of the island's network, but five years later, and after much effort, the Wight Locomotive Society made the Smallbrook Junction to Wootton section – of which Ashey is part – open to the public as a heritage railway, and trains have been running on the line ever since.

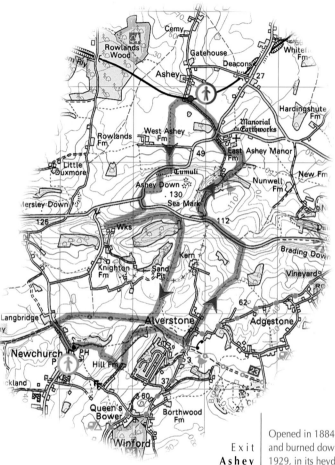

Exit **Ashey Station** and turn right on the track. Leave the track where it crosses the railway line to walk around the western perimeter of what was once Ashey Racecourse. ▶

Aim for and cross the road in the distance to take the footpath nearly opposite; turn right and almost

Opened in 1884 and burned down in 1929, in its heyday the racecourse attracted 3000 spectators for its thrice-annual meets and even had its own railway station.

171

immediately ascend two flights of steps up **Ashey Down**. Continue ascending beyond the steps, and when the **Sea Mark** comes into view cross a stile to head towards it (see Walk 32). After admiring the sensational panoramic view, turn right and continue on a faint path through the grass. Turn left on reaching a road and immediately left again on Brading Down Road, keeping to the grassy path. At the bend, follow footpath NC3 over a stile, and almost immediately bear right on the pathless grass next to a fence on your right, with an exceptional view south and southwest.

Having passed a trough in 350 metres, descend three-quarters-left to locate and cross a stile hidden in a fence. Turn left at the track below, which narrows to become a long but very pleasant path through this tranquil side-valley. On finally reaching a T-junction turn right. Cross the Bembridge Trail (1km) to continue on NC10, and in 450 metres ignore B53 branching left. A boardwalk soon leads over the marshy ground. Turn right at a T-junction with the concrete Yar River Trail (with the Eastern Yar on the left) and continue to the road at **Newchurch** (pub).

Turn left to walk up the hill towards the village centre. Shortly take NC11 running parallel to the road and look out for steps on the right that ascend to the churchyard. The village is beyond, but the onward route is to turn left to follow the churchyard wall. At the far end, return to and continue on your original path, but then immediately turn right on a permissive footpath, now entering lovely Martin's Wood and Newchurch Bee Fields. In 90 metres turn left onto the first obvious path (with benches just ahead), and at a path crossroads in 150 metres, by an information board, continue straight on. At a fork in a further 150 metres, bear half-right into the trees; turn right at the T-junction ahead and in 150 metres left into woodland, shortly crossing a stream and ascending a rise towards **Hill Farm** at the top.

Turn left through the farm, and in 200 metres descend left into a beautiful wood. Ignore a left turn after 200 metres and another path offshoot after a further 250 metres. In a further 150 metres, bear left, back into the

open, and continue towards, and through, a gate visible below. Shortly meet the Yar River Trail again and take B54 opposite, beside the Yar. Shortly after crossing the river by lovely Alverstone Mill, turn left on the lane to walk through **Alverstone**. In 150 metres keep ahead, soon branching off on B43 to maintain the same direction. Ignore ways off and ascend to the road over the downs; the gradient soon increases, but so does the scope of the vista towards Sandown Bay. Turn left at the road, with the view now north and west.

In 700 metres turn right on R26 to descend into Eaglehead and Bloodstone Copses.

Eastern Yar at Alverstone

> To all intents and purposes **Eaglehead and Bloodstone Copses** form one wood, and ancient woodland at that. Oak, ash and hazel are predominant and, as with much of the island's woodland, coppicing is practised, which increases nut production for the benefit of the red squirrels. Tits, owls and buzzards may also be seen.

Take the right fork at a junction after 850 metres, and in a further 350 metres bear left to enter another wood;

Ashey Station

Remember that Ashey is a request stop, so hold out your hand to stop the train.

ignore an immediate right fork to continue along the edge of a field. Look out for, and follow, a hidden left turn after 100 metres, crossing a steam. At the track at the end of the field, turn right to a road and take R29 almost opposite to return to **Ashey Station**. ◄

WALK 26

Ryde to Ventnor

Start	Ryde Esplanade Station
Finish	Ventnor
Distance	29.3km (18.3m)
Grade	Initially easy, but the walk becomes progressively harder; the final ascent up Wroxall Down is strenuous
Time	7½hr
Refreshments	A sprinkling of possibilities between Ryde and the Boat House pub at Spring Vale (2.5km); thereafter only Brading (9.2km) and Wroxall (25km)
Public transport	To start: bus routes 2, 3, 4, 8 and 9, and train; from finish: bus routes 3 and 6
Parking	Long-stay car parks in St Thomas Street, just west of the pier
Early finish	Pondwell (3.7km, bus route 8), Brading (9.2km, bus routes 2 and 3), Newport–Lake road (A3056) (19.2km, bus route 8), Newport–Shanklin road (A3020) (22km, bus route 2), Wroxall (25km, bus route 3)

This walk is perfect for Portsmouth day trippers who want to attempt a challenging coast to coast walk with continued interest and variety. But if the distance is too demanding, then Brading – home of the island's oldest house and several other curios – makes a convenient place to split the walk. As ever, the main draw is the scenery: views are simply stunning on top of Brading Down, and even more so from St Boniface Down on the descent to Ventnor. But the sheer variety of landscape is also an enticement, ranging from the initial Coastal Path section to lonely fields and centuries-old farms between Pondwell and Brading, picturesque bluebell woods alive with birdsong, and the final dramatic downland finish.

From the esplanade at **Ryde** (accommodation, supermarket, pubs, cafés, restaurants, shops, toilets), head east, soon passing some attractive

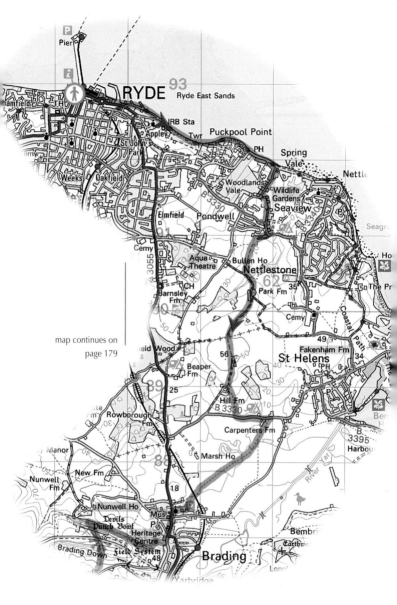

map continues on
page 179

Victorian villas, and continue following the coastline. Aim for **Appley Tower** in the distance (see Walk 9), and at the junction beyond it bear left to continue along the sea wall. At the café beside Puckpool Park, there is a choice of paths: through the park (converted from a land battery in 1928) or either of the parallel shore-side paths. All routes conjoin at the Boat House pub, the start of a 'suburb' of Seaview called **Spring Vale**.

Turn inland at the first opportunity (Oakhill Road), and in 450 metres turn left on footpath R59. On reaching a road in **Pondwell**, by bus stops, turn left, and after 150 metres turn right on R61. Having rounded an enclosure, cross a field and turn left at a T-junction, now on a wide track. Pass through rustic **Park Farm**, and 600 metres later go straight across a track onto B11, continuing to enjoy the quiet and solitude. Look behind for your last view of the Solent – at least for now.

Turn right at a T-junction with a track (400 metres) to head towards and through **Hill Farm**, with Brading and Sandown Bay now visible ahead, and descend to a road. Turn left and walk (carefully) for 400 metres, then turn right on B4 and walk half-right across the field

View from Brading Down towards Shanklin

ahead, aiming for the corner. Continue on B4 through the Brading Marshes Nature Reserve (see Walk 30); if or when the way seems unclear, always head towards Brading. Eventually cross first a railway line then almost immediately a hidden footbridge on your left; walk through the field ahead on a faint path, turning right at a road. Walk through the churchyard at **Brading** (pubs, restaurant/café, fish and chip shop, grocery store, toilets) and past the animal pound to emerge at the early Tudor Old Rectory Mansion, said to be the oldest house on the island. ◄

For those who wish to end the walk here, bus stops are situated to the right.

Walk down and then up the winding High Street, then up the secondary road ahead (The Mall). In 100 metres turn right into a surgery car park and continue into the park. Then immediately turn left uphill – a lovely scene of newly planted trees and (perhaps) wildflowers, and a wonderful view from the top towards Brading and beyond to Hill Farm which was passed earlier. Go through a gap in the treeline and turn right on the path beyond. Stay on the salient, undulating path ignoring ways off. You are now walking on Nunwell Down: rich, broadleaved ancient woodland and a joy to walk through.

After 1.3km – or 150 metres before a junction with a three-way signpost – bear sharp left on a narrower path, ascending and going back on yourself. Go through a gate near the top to leave the wood, and swing right using the main path across the field to cross the road at the top of the down and reach a sensational viewpoint on top of **Brading Down**.

From here the entire Sandown Bay coastline is visible, as is Brading Roman Villa. The down is a **Scheduled Ancient Monument** and host to the finest surviving ancient (Iron Age or Roman) field system on the island.

Descend the down via B42, with the view expanding to the west. In 200 metres turn right at a junction of paths to continue the descent through a wooden gate. On

map continues on
page 181

reaching a
road turn right, now in **Adgestone**, or more specifically
beside Adgestone vineyard, reputedly of Roman origin
and the oldest in Britain.

Stay on this very quiet and pleasant lane for 1km;
then, on the brow of a hill, turn left on B44 (ignore the
footpath over a stile shortly before it). Having descended
to another quiet lane turn right. Then just after 'Highleigh'
on the right (350 metres), take B51 left. Coming into the
open (150 metres), keep the field boundary on the right
initially, then the path swings left to cross in succession
a stream, the Eastern Yar and a track which was once the
railway line from Newport to Sandown and is now part of
the Yar River Trail.

At the next junction – opposite a sign for Skinners
Meadow – turn right, and in 150 metres right again
through Alverstone Mead Nature Reserve (look out for
the wildlife hide at the start of the path).

Alverstone Mead Nature Reserve is home to drag-
onflies, kingfishers, woodpeckers, herons, barn
owls and a host of other wildlife. Red squirrels may
also be spotted in the ancient woodland.

A long boardwalk soon leads out onto a lane near
Alverstone. Take a short detour right to see the pretty

179

*Alverstone Mead
Nature Reserve*

*Borthwood Copse,
a corruption of
'Broadwood', is the
first of a series of
bluebell-carpeted
woods south of
Alverstone, most
likely a surviving
part of ancient
hunting forest.*

Eastern Yar flow through the hamlet; otherwise cross the lane and continue on NC42, staying with the footpath in 250 metres. Reach and cross a lane to continue on NC4. At the lane through the hamlet of **Queen's Bower** – named after the last Lord of the Isle of Wight, Lady Isabella de Fortibus – turn left, in 80 metres descending an unmarked and inconspicuous footpath into Borthwood Copse. ◄

At a crossroads in 150 metres, turn right slightly uphill. Stay on this main path, ignoring all ways off your current direction (which is nearly due south). After 600 metres exit the wood completely and come out into the open to continue on a broad grassy path. Keep ahead at a four-armed signpost and turn right at the field corner. Cross a drive to the left to locate and follow a narrow path ahead that emerges on the Newport–Lake road (A3056) with bus stops nearby. Descend NC37 opposite, through another delightful but potentially boggy stretch of woodland.

At a crossroads (700 metres), continue on NC37 through a field, with America Wood below and the downland still to climb beyond. Descend steps into more woodland, and after another potentially boggy stretch officially enter **America Wood** (see Walk 22). At a junction 70 metres from the barrier, turn right on a narrow path to start a semi-circuit of the wood's northern half. In 500 metres ignore a right turn, and shortly afterwards – at a wooden barrier with a stone house ahead – turn right along a wide track through the southern portion of the wood.

Stay on this main track, eventually emerging on the Newport–Shanklin road (A3020) (closest bus stops to your right), and take NC39 opposite. Cross the former Shanklin–Ventnor railway line to continue over a stile. Cross a second stile (200 metres) and a third immediately on your right to ascend half-left over the pathless grass, aiming for the crest of the hill just to the right of the trees ahead (a steep, strenuous climb, but with a wonderful view soon behind you).

map continues on page 182

When there, cross the stile ahead and maintain your current direction to cross three stiles bunched together. Continue just 40 metres to the foot of the hillock ahead and turn right on a faint level path. On entering another field, keep ahead on the main, level path. Keep to the left of a fence (150 metres), cross a stile (400 metres) and turn left to enter a wood. Continue at the crossroads along V34, and in 300 metres, with a view of Appuldurcombe House in the valley ahead, bear left through a gate onto a wide grassy path. In 100m ignore the wide ascending path, taking the narrow level path instead. Gradually descend and ignore ways off. On reaching a small green facing the

181

church at
Wroxall (limited
accommodation, pub,
grocery store), bear left. ◀

*Alternatively, for
refreshments or to
shorten the walk,
continue over the
bridge to the main
road and bus stops.*

Turn left into St Martin's Road, and in 100 metres turn
right on a concrete path, continuing on grass just past
the playground. Once over a second stream, ignore ways
off for 350 metres then, just after a second metal gate,
turn left uphill with the track, shortly swinging right. After
a further 200 metres go through another gate and turn
right along a pretty grassy path with lovely wildflowers

Wood on Wroxall Down

in spring. Reach Wroxall Cross near a bridge over the former Shanklin–Ventnor railway line. Turn left to take a private road (not Middle Barn Lane), and continue on a drive after 40 metres (V8) to start the increasingly steep climb up Wroxall Down, with a particularly pleasant wooded section near the top.

On eventually reaching the ridge turn left along the drive, and after 200 metres turn right on V1a. ▶ At the end of the path, facing the shimmering sea, turn right onto V1 to commence the most spectacular section of the walk. In 200 metres ignore the path curving clockwise to continue ahead over the grass, keeping the sea to your left and a steep-sided valley to your right; houses in Ventnor can be seen nestling in the greenery ahead.

The island's highest point is at the nearby radar station: 241m (791ft) above sea level.

After a while descend steeply, soon finding steps. At the bottom of the slope descend more steps, eventually emerging in an industrial estate that was once Ventnor Station. To continue to the town centre, cross the road ahead to descend Grove Road and take the first right (Tulse Hill). Emerge at the bus stop in High Street in **Ventnor** (accommodation, supermarkets, pubs, cafés, restaurants, shops, toilets), but if you wish to take 'coast to coast' literally continue another few hundred metres to the seafront.

WALK 27
Seaview circular

Start/Finish	Centre of Seaview
Distance	19.9km (12.4 miles)
Grade	Moderate
Time	5hr
Refreshments	St Helens (2.6km), Lord Yarborough Monument (9km), Bembridge Point (15.1km)
Public transport	Bus route 8
Parking	Car park in Pier Road
Early finish	St Helens (2.6km, bus route 8), foot of Gander Down (7.1km, bus route 8), Whitecliff Bay (11.5km and 12.6km, bus route 8), Bembridge Point (15.1km, bus route 8)

Some of the island's hidden gems (or at least hidden to tourists) are revealed on this greatly rewarding walk. The overlooked village of Seaview has some of the most interesting residence exteriors on the island, especially by the shoreline. Beyond is St Helens which, uniquely for the island, is centred around a village green, apparently the second-largest in England. The relatively low height of Gander Down belies the rare view of Brading from its summit, while Bembridge and Culver Downs provide sensational views of Sandown and Whitecliff Bays. A walk through pretty Steyne Wood brings you to a windmill (National Trust) on the outskirts of Bembridge, after which the official Coastal Path is followed, slightly inland, back to Seaview.

From the top of High Street at **Seaview** (limited accommodation, pub, cafés, restaurants, shops, toilets), head east on Pier Road to pass the car park and descend towards the sea. Choose either route at the fork: they will merge again shortly and you will eventually arrive on the shoreline at Seagrove Bay. Walk a few paces seaward for the view then return to ascend steeply, shortly passing some intriguing properties.

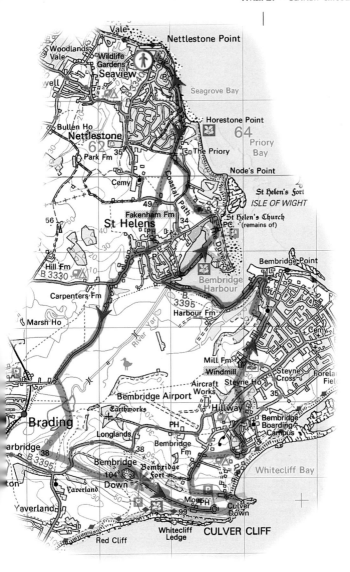

Pass the entrance to the **Priory Bay Hotel**, go over a stile, and continue along the left side of a field. On walking through a second field, notice the tower of St Helens Church peeking through the trees on your right.

St Helens Church was built in 1717 to replace its recently disused predecessor by the sea (passed on Walk 9). In those days the parish included what is now Seaview and even eastern Ryde. The church was almost completely rebuilt in the 1830s.

At a road, cross to the right and continue on footpath R82. Ignore a right fork in 550 metres to emerge opposite the village green of **St Helens** (pub, cafés, restaurants, shops, toilets).

St Helens has its origins in Saxon times, when it was probably called Etharin. Originally centred on the area known as the Duver ('duver' is an island word for sand dunes), a wooden church was constructed there in the eighth century but destroyed in 998. Then in the 1080s a Benedictine Priory, dedicated to St Helena, was established approximately where today's Priory Bay Hotel stands. A French invasion was repelled in 1340, and six years later it was from here that Edward III left to successfully invade Normandy. Nelson too departed from St Helens, for the Battle of Trafalgar, and it is said that the village was his last view of England. The village green is a conservation area – the cottages are mainly 18th century and very few properties have been built since the Second World War.

The railway was in operation from 1882 to 1953, and ran frequent trains between Bembridge and Brading, calling also at St Helens.

Turn right on the road and keep to this direction until the bottom of the hill. Shortly after the pavement ends turn left on B56 (known as Laundry Lane) along the former Bembridge–Brading railway branch line, which soon enters Brading Marshes Nature Reserve (see Walk 30). ◄

In 950 metres, take a footpath to the right, running parallel to the track. Where the path rejoins the track, go

through a gate and turn left at the junction ahead (B3), keeping the hedgerow on your left; cross one branch of the Eastern Yar (400 metres), followed by another (150 metres). Immediately afterwards take the right fork to go through a swing gate and ascend Gander Down all the way to the top where, despite being just 39m (128ft) high, there is a marvellous panoramic view, including a rather special perspective of the houses of Brading, nestling on a hillside. Notice Brading Station below the church.

Brading from Gander Down

From the summit, head directly towards Bembridge Fort (on top of the hill to your right as you face the sea). Soon gates should be seen below; aim for and cross them, and cross the road ahead to take BB44. ▸ Leave the footpath almost immediately, bearing half-left to steeply ascend **Bembridge Down** (no path). Once at **Bembridge Fort**, skirt clockwise around it, the view now towards St Helens, Bembridge Airport and Harbour, and a swathe of the mainland's south coast.

Bus stops are 5min walk to the right.

Bembridge Fort is a 'Palmerston Folly', built in the 1860s in response to a perceived threat of French invasion. It served a more practical purpose during

187

the Second World War as home to an anti-aircraft unit and local headquarters of the Home Guard. The National Trust purchased the fort in the 1960s and tours are available by arrangement.

Head towards the Lord Yarborough Monument (see Walk 9) when it becomes visible (still staying just below the ridge), eventually emerging onto a drive. Go through a gap in the hedge opposite and turn left to keep following the ridge on grass, now back with the magnificent view of Sandown Bay. Stay on the grass until you are led back onto the drive and continue along it, past the **Culver Haven Inn** (which could be immensely useful in adverse weather). ◀

The information board just past the pub states that the first wireless signal station on the south coast was erected here in 1900.

Descend to reach Culver Battery (another fortification, completed in 1906) and continue how you wish towards the sea (now on the **Culver Down** peninsula), until the protective clifftop fence prevents any further progress. Turn left to follow the fence in the direction of Whitecliff Bay. At a second corner, with a fantastic view of the eroded Whitecliff Bay cliffs, bear sharp left on an ascending faint grassy path. Keep to your current

Atop Culver Down looking towards Bembridge

Lord Yarborough Monument

direction, with the fence always nearby on your right. Go through a gate and continue back towards the **Lord Yarborough Monument**.

When there – or when level with the Culver Haven – descend the slope obliquely, still heading away from Whitecliff Bay, soon to find and follow a stony track descending the down. Ignore ways off to cross a field and then descend a lane to reach Glovers Farm. A further 200 metres along the lane turn right abruptly on BB17. ▶ At a T-junction inside a holiday park turn right, keeping a fence on your right, and walk around the holiday homes. Turn left just past the crazy golf course and at a crossroads of sorts continue ahead to keep the majority of holiday homes on the right.

In 70 metres branch into woodland, and at the end of the path turn left to reach the road. ▶ Turn right and, in 200 metres, left (BB22), soon entering Steyne Wood, a relatively unspoiled area of ancient woodland. Cross the next road, bear right in 100 metres, and ascend towards **Bembridge Windmill** (see Walk 30). Maintain the current direction at the windmill and road ahead, and turn left on reaching the road (in effect, straight on), now in

Alternatively, continue to the end of the lane to find bus stops.

Bus stops are on the left.

Bembridge (limited accommodation, supermarket, pubs, cafés, restaurants, shops, toilets).

Look out for, and follow, BB3 on your left (550 metres). ◄ Ignore ways off and emerge onto the harbour road. A detour into Beach Road opposite will reward with a 180-degree sea view at **Bembridge Point.** To return to Seaview, continue around **Bembridge Harbour**. Cross the Eastern Yar (1.3km) and take the first right (Latimer Road). Branch off right after 100 metres, shortly following the sea wall, which becomes a delightful causeway through the harbour. It is possible you will have just the seabirds for company.

At the end of the causeway continue on the grass through **St Helens Duver** (see Walk 9) and make your way towards the pillared Old Club House ahead on the left. At the road junction just past it, take R85 (opposite) through two fields, linked by a footbridge over a stream (bear left just after it). Ascend the second field and exit its far right corner to turn right into a lane and soon bear left into the drive of the **Priory Bay Hotel**. A footpath shortly branches away from the drive, and in 300 metres swing right with the main path to retrace the walk's initial section down to **Seagrove Bay** and the short seaside stroll back to **Seaview**.

Continue along the road for the village shops.

WALK 28
Wootton Bridge circular

Start/Finish	Wootton Bridge, opposite the Sloop Inn
Distance	17.9km (11.2 miles)
Grade	Fairly easy
Time	4½hr
Refreshments	Havenstreet (12.7km), Quarr Abbey (15.5km), Fishbourne (15.7km)
Public transport	Bus routes 4 and 9
Parking	Lakeside Hotel or the Sloop Inn (customers only). The car park in Brannon Way is short stay.
Early finish	Near Quarr Abbey (15.1km, bus routes 4 and 9)

This consistently lovely walk is replete with trees, so do it when they are in full leaf. It dips into three of the numerous ancient woods surrounding the village of Havenstreet and features the seductive sight and sound of steam trains on the Isle of Wight Steam Railway. It might be a good idea, then, to do this walk when the railway is running; the route twice crosses the line, and in summer you won't have to wait long to see the trains. Note that this walk is not possible during the annual 'Bestival' music festival in early September.

From **Wootton Bridge** (limited accommodation, supermarket, pubs, restaurants, shops, toilets) take bridleway N1 heading south, with the lake (Old Mill Pond) on the left. In 100 metres branch right, shortly bear left, and in 350 metres cross a stile on the left to enter Hurst Copse. At the end of a boardwalk, bear left for a short detour to a secluded part of the lake, then return to continue along the other fork, which leads back to the original track, now opposite a former ice house. Turn left to continue along this pleasant bridleway, eventually crossing the steam railway line for the first time.

Steam train crossing the route

In the colder months or after wet weather, the wood may be prohibitively boggy, in which case continue along the road and turn into the wood further on to continue the walk.

Continue on a stony track to a T-junction and turn left (N15). At the far end of **Great Briddlesford Farm** go through a metal gate to continue on a path between hedgerows. Emerge onto a road, then turn right and almost immediately left on an inconspicuous path now inside **Combley Great Wood**. ◀ Turn right at a junction of paths beside a group of conifers (150 metres); then in 600 metres, with a path coming in from the left, bear right and almost immediately sharp left on a track to continue to a T-junction at the far side of the wood. Turn left and then right at another T-junction. The fields soon passed host 'Bestival', the nationally famous music festival.

Bear left through **Combley Farm** (850 metres) and in a further 250 metres, just before a cattle grid, turn sharp left to ascend one field and left again on a track inside a second. Continue through two more fields and keep to your current direction on a track. At a junction after 300 metres swing right, shortly passing **Duxmore Farm** on your left to ascend in your current direction. At a junction of paths by a house continue uphill on the stony track, eventually reaching a lane. Turn left and immediately right (R22), with a grand view ahead towards Ashey Sea Mark.

Aim for the nearside fence to the left of the copse ahead and go through the gate to enter another field. Bear half-left, still with no path, never straying far from the left field edge. Go through another gate in the far side of the field and

Kemphill Moor Copse

continue in your current direction – a lovely rural scene. Keep the field boundary on the left – including long gaps in the hedgerow – and re-cross the stream railway line to pick up a faint grassy path. In 350 metres turn left on a signposted footpath and soon enter the enchanting, mostly coniferous Kemphill Moor Copse.

Ignore the initial right fork and keep to the main path, eventually leaving the wood and continuing to a lane to take a right turn. Take the first lane on the left and turn right at a T-junction, now in the village of **Havenstreet** (pub). ◀ Turn right at the next T-junction and, at the junction with Firestone Copse Road, take R5 ahead and ascend the hillock towards a large First World War **memorial** at the top.

For the pub turn left at this junction.

Cross to the next field, with the mainland now in view, and continue in the same direction through more fields to pass to the right of **Newnham Farm** and onto a lane, still keeping to your current direction. Bear left in 70 metres through a gate and continue diagonally across the field towards another gate, just visible. Cross it to continue beside a lake. On reaching the main road just east of **Fishbourne** turn left to find bus stops; or to

continue the walk, cross the road to follow R4a. In 150 metres, turn left onto the signposted 'Woodland Walk', emerging onto the Coastal Path near the entrance to **Quarr Abbey.** Turn left on the track, passing the abbey on the right. At a T-junction by The Fishbourne pub turn left, pass Fishbourne ferry terminal, and 250 metres further turn right on the signposted footpath and left at the T-junction – now with occasional views towards Wootton Creek. Where the lane swings left, go straight ahead on a track signed to 'The Plantation'. Ascend to the main road and turn right to return back to **Wootton Bridge**.

Lake near Fishbourne

WALK 29

Wootton Bridge to Newport

Start	Wootton Bridge, opposite the Sloop Inn
Finish	Newport bus station
Distance	10.3km (6.4 miles)
Grade	Easy
Time	2½hr
Refreshments	Wootton (2.1km), Island Harbour Marina (6.4km)
Public transport	To start: bus routes 4 and 9; from finish: bus routes 1, 2, 3, 5, 6, 7, 8, 9 and 12
Parking	Lakeside Hotel or the Sloop Inn (customers only). The car park in Brannon Way is short stay.
Early finish	Nowhere on the route is far from the main road, from where there are frequent buses

The path along the eastern bank of the Medina estuary has recently been reinforced to accommodate bikes, and strolling along it is a tranquil and enjoyable way to approach Newport. The prelude to the riverside section crosses the steam railway heritage line near Wootton Station and continues on the line's former course, before walking round the edges of Fattingpark Copse and reaching Island Harbour Marina midway along the estuary. Heading into Newport town centre is no less agreeable, via two of its most interesting streets (Quay Street and Watchbell Lane) and some of its notable buildings (particularly the Guildhall).

From **Wootton Bridge** (limited accommodation, supermarket, pubs, restaurants, shops, toilets) take bridleway N1 heading south, with the lake (Old Mill Pond) on your left. In 100 metres branch right, then shortly bear right again along a drive and cycle track (signposted to Fernhill Park). Emerge at, and continue along, a residential street to a more major road. Turn left, then almost immediately left again into Packsfield Lane, which soon becomes a

track. Look out for **Wootton Station** – a steam railway terminus – on your right.

Cross the railway line and bear right (N6) to ascend to a road at **Wootton Common** and here turn left, immediately passing a pub. ▶ Turn right at the roundabout and right again just after 'Quarrels Copse' in 150 metres, along a grassy path between gardens. Continue through a wood, maintaining the current direction and ignoring path offshoots. On reaching a T-junction, turn left on the former railway track, which is an extension of the current preserved steam railway crossed earlier. ▶

Cross a road to continue on the old railway track. At a track crossroads (500 metres) turn left into Fattingpark Copse. Continuing along the track would be the most direct route, and is advised in muddy conditions, but this circuitous option adds a bit more diversity. Where the main track swings right (200 metres), continue in your current direction. In a further 250 metres swing right with the main path along the edge of the wood, at the end of which turn right (N115), shortly with the first splendid view of the Medina.

Crossing the steam railway

Continue ahead for bus stops.

Trains used to run along here from Ryde to Cowes via Newport, and this stretch – from Wootton to Newport – is considered the most likely candidate for restoration.

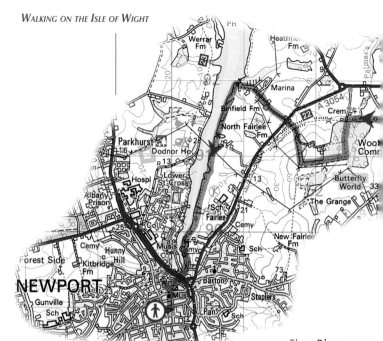

The **River Medina** estuary ('Medina' is a corruption of the Saxon *medene*, meaning 'middle river'), which runs from Newport to Cowes, is so prominent, especially when viewed on the map, that most people probably don't realise that the 17km-long river actually rises from the north face of St Catherine's Down, some distance to the south of Newport. As with all island rivers, the estuary mudflats and saltmarsh attract a wide variety of birds, both resident (such as mallards, mute swans, coot) and over-wintering (such as Brent geese, widgeon, teal). In the 18th and 19th centuries the estuary provided a resting place for vessels transporting convicts to Australia.

At a T-junction with a track (650 metres), turn left to go under the railway track (the same one as before) to

reach a main road. ▶ Cross here to continue along N121, which arrives at **Island Harbour Marina**.

The nearest bus stops are some way along on the left.

The East Medina tidal mill was built at **Island Harbour Marina** in 1790 and was used until 1939, additionally serving as barracks during the early 1800s to house friendly foreign soldiers and French PoWs after the Napoleonic Wars. The building was demolished in 1950 after a major fire, to be replaced by the marina in the mid-1960s. Look out for The Tide Mill House on the right just before the marina; it was built for the original mill owner in 1790.

Beside the Medina

Looking towards Newport

The once-esteemed 1930s paddle-steamer Ryde Queen has been lying derelict here for decades now, scandalously rusting away.

Continue to the river bank and turn left to start the riverside meander towards **Newport**. ◀ In 1.8km notice the trees of Newport Arboretum to the left. Soon after passing a hotel and restaurant, emerge on a drive at the start of Newport Quay.

Continue along the quayside and walk under the road bridge. This is now the start of the estuary, fed by the Medina flowing in from the left, and another tributary – Lukely Brook – from the right. Pass the Grade II listed Dolphin Inn to continue up Quay Street.

> **Quay Street** is arguably the most elegant and evocative street in Newport, full of 17th- and 18th-century town houses and small, charming hotels. It was constructed as part of Richard de Redvers' original 12th-century town layout and would have been the entrance to the town for those arriving by boat. At the top of Quay Street is the neoclassical Grade II listed Guildhall: built by John Nash and finished in 1816, it hosts the very informative Museum of Island History.

A the top of the street turn sharp right down quaint Watchbell Lane, sharp left at the end of the short parade, and go straight across the crossroads, keeping the minster on your right. Carry on across another crossroads to come to a major junction. Newport bus station is on Orchard Street to your right.

WALK 30
Bembridge Trail

Start	Newport bus station
Finish	Bembridge Point
Distance	20.1km (12.6 miles)
Grade	Fairly easy after a moderate ascent
Time	5½hr
Refreshments	Arreton (5.2km), Brading (14.8km)
Public transport	To start: bus routes 1, 2, 3, 5, 6, 7, 8, 9 and 12; from finish: bus route 8
Parking	The nearest long-stay car park is a 5min walk away – at Coppins Bridge, near the multiplex
Early finish	Arreton (5.1km, bus route 8 and seasonal Downs Breezer), Knighton (8.5km, Downs Breezer), Brading (14.9km, bus routes 2 and 3)

The Bembridge Trail is one of the island's official trails. Meandering across the east of the island from capital to coast, it follows and shadows the downland stretching roughly between Newport and Brading – sometimes on the ridge, sometimes in the valley – and there is always something attractive in sight to maintain interest. The Brading to Bembridge section resembles something of a coda; quite different to what has gone before, it initially traverses potentially boggy Brading Marshes – the only RSPB nature reserve on the island – before ascending via recently re-laid footpaths to Bembridge Windmill and the final stretch to Bembridge Point. A short and pleasant prelude beside the Medina is included to enable a start from central Newport.

From **Newport** bus station head east along South Street and take the third right (Furrlongs), turning right again on footpath N218 (80 metres). Keep the River Medina on the right, in 700 metres crossing it and turning left to reach a road. Cross the adjacent main road and take St Georges Lane ahead, following a signpost for byway A28 and

ascend-
ing **St
George's
Down** – now
at the official start
of the Bembridge Trail.

The lane starts to gain
height, and height usually implies
views, in this case a panorama of the centre of the island
from the Solent to St Catherine's Down. Once at the top
of the lane continue along the track ahead, soon beside
a golf course. Ignore ways off the main track – bright-
ened by gorse in season – and, shortly after it starts to
descend (2km from its start), at a three-armed signpost,
turn left and immediately right over a stile. This is a minor
but very worthwhile deviation from the official trail on
account of the view.

Spot the village down below (Arreton), and descend
the pathless grass towards it. Find a gap in the bracken

leading to a stile and descend along the edge of two fields (sweet-smelling rapeseed in May) towards a road. Take A27a opposite, leading to the shops and eateries of **Arreton Barns**. Turn left on the adjacent road, pass bus stops, and turn left into School Lane 100 metres past the pub. Take either parallel fork shortly ahead, but when they converge keep to the left of the hedgerow. At a track T-junction beside an artificial lake, turn right and immediately left, still in the shadow of the downs to the north. Notice the church of Newchurch on the hillside to the southeast.

map continues on page 204

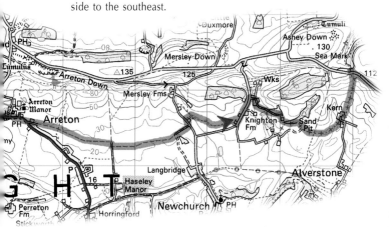

Ignore ways off until a five-way path junction (850 metres). Take either of the parallel tracks ahead – both ascend to a lane where the walk turns left. Turn right on NC1 (60 metres) and swing right with the track.

At a road turn left, soon passing bus stops. This is **Knighton**, located in a beautiful and very green little pocket of the island – a riot of colour in the autumn. Turn right 200 metres from the bus stops (NC45). In a further 500 metres, with Harts Ash Farm visible ahead, turn right on a wide track with overhanging branches. Ignore ways off this lovely, winding track; then, in 1.1km,

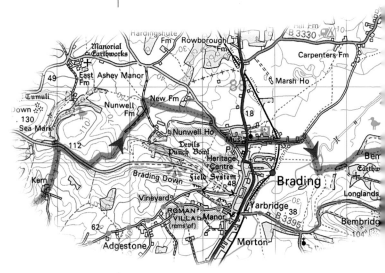

beside another farm, take B35 sharp right, initially away from the farm. In 90 metres turn left (B33a), and once on the other side of the farm stay on the main track, continuing to ascend the down. Soon Shanklin and Sandown Bay come into view. Cross the road at the top of the down and turn right, soon with a wonderful northerly view.

Turn left on B26 (600 metres), and at the foot of the descent turn left through a gate to follow the grassy path ahead. Keep to the main path, which eventually descends to **Nunwell Farm**. At a T-junction just past the farm turn left, and in 150 metres go right (B23) over the pathless grass following the direction indicated by the signpost. At the top of the giant second field head towards a fence just visible ahead on the left, soon noticing **Nunwell House** to the right, in the shadow of Brading Down.

A beautiful house set in equally beautiful gardens, **Nunwell House** was the Oglander family's residence

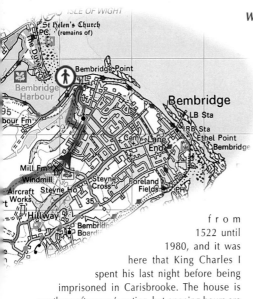

from 1522 until 1980, and it was here that King Charles I spent his last night before being imprisoned in Carisbrooke. The house is worth an afternoon's outing, but opening hours are limited.

Pass to the right of the farm, which the fence encloses, and continue through a third field towards the village of Brading. On reaching a road turn right with care, passing the Nunwell House driveway and bearing right into Doctors Lane a little further ahead. At a junction inside the village, bear left down Cross Street to reach the centre of **Brading** (pubs, restaurant/café, fish and chip shop, grocery store, toilets), next to the Lilliput Antique Doll and Toy Museum.

Turn right for the pubs and village store, otherwise left. Turn into Quay Lane, just before the church, to pass Old Rectory Mansion, reputedly the oldest house on the island and recently turned into a popular restaurant/café. ▶ At the end of the lane, continue on B3, now in **Brading Marshes Nature Reserve**. Keep the hedgerow on your left and cross one branch of the Eastern Yar (400 metres) followed by another (150 metres). Be sure to bear left at the junction shortly after this second branch.

Alternatively, to end the walk here continue past the church to reach bus stops.

Crossing the Eastern Yar, Brading Marshes Nature Reserve

Brading Marshes Nature Reserve was originally an extension of today's Bembridge Harbour. The enlarged area was known as Brading Harbour or Brading Haven. It was only in 1878 that the building of an embankment from Bembridge to St Helens 'turned sea into land'. It is the island's sole RSPB reserve, although by no means its sole bird magnet (other popular spots include Newtown Harbour). Ironically, man's drainage methods have arguably become too successful, and the RSPB is working to retain a distinct wetland environment for the benefit of wading birds and their admirers. Birds that might be seen include buzzards, warblers and lapwings (spring), woodpeckers and wagtails (summer), swallows and house martins (autumn), and widgeon and yellowhammer (winter). Buzzards and owls may also be spotted. The small areas of woodland in the centre of the reserve, such as Centurion's Copse, are termed 'ancient' (in existence before 1600) and provide a haven for red squirrels as well as playing host to daffodils, primroses, celandines, violets and bluebells.

At the next path junction (350 metres), bear left on BB20 then turn left at the T-junction ahead, soon emerging back into the open. Keep to the main path, with Bembridge Fort and the Lord Yarborough Monument soon visible on the right and the village of St Helens on the left. On crossing into a second field, **Bembridge Windmill** becomes visible on the rise ahead – the path keeps heading towards it.

> **Bembridge Windmill** was in operation between 1700 and 1913 and is the last remaining windmill on the island, still containing much of its original machinery. Turner painted it during his visit to the island in 1795. One of many 1960s island acquisitions by the National Trust, it may be visited between mid-March and late October.

Turn left at the T-junction beside the entrance, and maintain your current direction at the road ahead, now in **Bembridge** (limited accommodation, supermarket, pubs, cafés, restaurants, shops, toilets).

Bembridge Windmill

Continue along the road for the village shops.

Look out for, and follow, BB3 on your left (550 metres). ◄ Ignore ways off and emerge onto the harbour road. Turn left for the bus stops, perhaps enjoying refreshments at the pub or café while waiting, or turn up Beach Road for a wonderful sea view at **Bembridge Point**.

WALK 31
Worsley Trail

Start	Three Bishops pub, Brighstone
Finish	Shanklin Old Village
Distance	21.7km (13.6 miles)
Grade	Moderate
Time	5½hr
Refreshments	Shorwell (4.3km – just off route), Godshill (14km), Wroxall (18.3km)
Public transport	To start: bus route 12; from finish: bus routes 2 and 3, and train
Parking	Warnes Lane car park (behind the Three Bishops pub)
Early finish	Shorwell (4.3km, bus route 12), near Chillerton (7.3km, bus route 6), Godshill (14km, bus routes 2 and 3), Wroxall (17.9km, bus route 3)
Note	The official starting point of the trail, at the National Trust car park on the Brighstone–Calbourne road, has no direct access by bus, and the initial section duplicates the Tennyson Trail, so an alternative start from Brighstone has been chosen and is, in fact, one of the highlights of the walk.

The Worsley Trail provides a link between the downland of the Back of the Wight and the southeast downland – the only walk in this book to do so. Views from both are spectacular and wide-reaching. In between is often pretty countryside, well off the beaten track, with pockets of interest such as remote New Barn Farm beneath the majesty of the Chillerton Down transmitter. The saccharine-sweet village of Godshill is also accessible via a short detour.

From the Three Bishops in **Brighstone** (limited accommodation, pub, restaurant/café, shops, toilets), walk towards the newsagent and turn right up pretty North Street, with its library and a museum. At the T-junction turn right

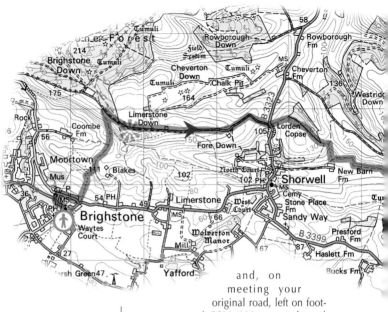

map continues on
page 212

*Toposcope atop
Limerstone Down*

and, on
meeting your
original road, left on footpath BS30 (200 metres); the path soon
starts to ascend the visible downland ahead. At the path
T-junction at the top turn left to head for the bulk that
is Limerstone Down. Ignore ways off and eventually the
path swings left to obliquely ascend the down.

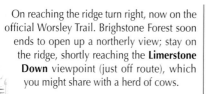

On reaching the ridge turn right, now on the official Worsley Trail. Brighstone Forest soon ends to open up a northerly view; stay on the ridge, shortly reaching the **Limerstone Down** viewpoint (just off route), which you might share with a herd of cows.

There is a glorious two-coast **panoramic view** from here, as well as a toposcope showing directions and distances to various towns in Britain and northern France.

Continue along the ridge, with stupendous views north and south, and stay on the track to reach a road in a few kilometres. Cross this and take SW49 opposite. ▶ Walk around two sides of a vast field before being led through a gate and swinging left with the track. On meeting another track turn sharp right towards isolated **New Barn Farm** in the valley. Just before the farm gate, turn left over the pathless grass, soon passing a signpost and ascending very steeply. Continue around the base of Northcourt Down and **Chillerton Down**, always ignoring ways off the salient grassy path, now in remotest countryside below the 230m (755ft) transmitter (see Walk 10).

Eventually a road is reached. Turn right, then left onto Berry Lane by bus stops at the top of the hill, and right at a T-junction after 900 metres. Turn left on G14 (150 metres), and on reaching a lane continue in the same direction, with **Cridmore Farm** on the right. Soon swing left with the lane, and at the end of the farm buildings continue in the same direction. After crossing a field and entering a second, immediately turn right with the path, soon crossing an infant **River Medina** and walking through a short wooded section.

Keep a hedgerow on your left, meet a track in 700 metres, and in a further 100 metres turn left by a signpost. Take the first opportunity to emerge onto the road, turn

Alternatively, turn right for a 30min return detour into Shorwell, where there is a pub, shop and bus stops.

211

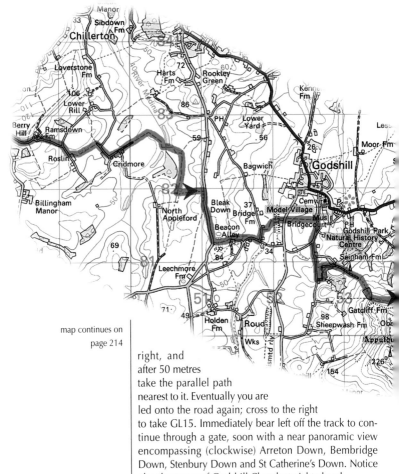

map continues on
page 214

right, and
after 50 metres
take the parallel path
nearest to it. Eventually you are
led onto the road again; cross to the right
to take GL15. Immediately bear left off the track to continue through a gate, soon with a near panoramic view
encompassing (clockwise) Arreton Down, Bembridge
Down, Stenbury Down and St Catherine's Down. Notice
also the tower of Godshill Church straight ahead.

Descend the meadow to a gate and continue towards
Godshill. Keep to the right edge of this field and the next,
at the end of which turn right through a gate to descend
to a lane. Turn left and soon left again (Bagwich Lane),
in 150 metres turning right on GL21. Fork right in 200
metres, shortly crossing the Eastern Yar in woodland
and abruptly arriving at, and skirting round, a delightful
pond inhabited by (at the time of writing at least) some

particularly noisy ducks! Cross a road to continue ahead, and at the next lane turn right. ▶

Shortly after a lane comes in from the left, turn left on Sheepwash Lane and in 450 metres left again on GL56. Ignore the descending path by **Sainham Farm** to go over a stile, and in 400 metres, with field gates on your left and right, take the main fork half-right to ascend towards trees. Then at a major path junction (400 metres) bear left uphill between a wire fence and a hedge, soon with a comprehensive view north and a stone wall on your right, once the boundary wall of the Appuldurcombe estate. Descend to, and walk through, neoclassical Freemantle Gate (see Walk 20), and after just 100 metres branch off the track towards the village of Wroxall below, ignoring ways off.

Time and energy permitting, however, it is worth making the 15min return detour to baroque **Appuldurcombe House**, further along the ridge. Once the grandest house on the island and with grounds landscaped by

Alternatively, go left for a few hundred metres to detour into the popular, photogenic village of Godshill (pubs, cafés, shops, toilets) for refreshments and bus stops.

Appuldurcombe House

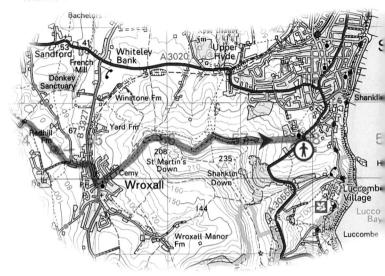

Capability Brown, it was built for the noble and influential Worsley family between 1701 and 1770. A 12th-century priory once stood on the site, so it is perhaps apt that the house was used by a Benedictine order about a century ago before a permanent home was found for them at Quarr Abbey. Now owned by English Heritage, the house contains a small permanent exhibition, although sadly the interior itself is in ruins following a Second World War bombing raid. Next to the house is an owl and falconry centre.

Emerging on a drive turn left, and right at the next junction, soon reaching the main road through **Wroxall** (limited accommodation, pub, grocery store) beside bus stops.

Wroxall is idyllically situated in a valley with the southeast downs on three sides, and consequently in the centre of prime walking country. It was a

relatively remote agricultural village before the advent of the railway in 1866, at which time the village was extended to accommodate the railway workers. The parish church was built some 10 years later with stone bored from the railway tunnel to Ventnor.

Ascend the rightmost of the two sets of steps across the road and turn right on the former Shanklin–Ventnor railway line at the top to reach a bridge close to the village church and pub. Wroxall Station used to be just across the road, but today there is no trace of it. Cross the bridge and bear left up Castle Road, branching right on V30 just beyond **Wroxall Cemetery**. In 500 metres, now on the lower slopes of **St Martin's Down**, bear right over a stile to enter a field and start walking clockwise around it. In a further 200 metres pass a memorial stone for Cook's Castle.

Cook's Castle was nothing more than an 18th-century folly erected by Capability Brown as part of his commission by Sir Richard Worsley to improve the Appuldurcombe estate. It was demolished in the middle of the 20th century.

Stray into a wood, and ignore ways off the fairly level path until you are led back out into the open. Bear half-left following a just-discernible path, with a truly sensational view opening up of Sandown Bay and the ridge of downland from Culver Down westwards. In about 100 metres bear left through the meadow towards the trees, again on the faintest of paths, and beyond a gate keep the steep incline just to the left. Eventually your path starts the grand descent towards **Shanklin**. Emerge in the delightful churchyard of Shanklin Old Church. ▶

For the centre of Shanklin (accommodation, supermarket, pubs, cafés, restaurants, shops, toilets) turn left on the road. The bus stops (route 3) are 250 metres away, just before the Old Village.

WALK 32
Shorwell to Brading

Start	Crown Inn, Shorwell
Finish	Brading
Distance	22.4km (14 miles)
Grade	Moderate
Time	6½hr
Refreshments	Arreton (12.1km)
Public transport	To start: bus route 12; from finish: bus routes 2 and 3, and train
Parking	B3323 or Crown Inn car park (customers only)
Early finish	Near Chillerton (3km, bus route 6), Rookley (6.8km, bus route 3), Merstone (10.1km, bus route 2), Arreton (11.9km, bus route 8 and seasonal Downs Breezer), Knighton (16.8km and seasonal Downs Breezer)

This long walk traverses two under-explored stretches of downland: to the east of Shorwell and the east of Arreton. Both villages have something to offer the visitor too: Shorwell its thatched cottages and woodland setting, and Arreton its touristy but tasteful Barns Craft Village and church with Saxon features. There are ample opportunities to shorten the walk, but plenty of stunning views make it well worth staying to the end. Choose a day when a southwesterly is blowing to help drive you along.

From the Crown Inn in **Shorwell** (limited accommodation, pub, shop), head east past the church and village store. Just beyond the latter, turn right onto footpath SW13. The path rises almost immediately; shortly Shorwell can be glimpsed nestling below the trees on the right and a marvellous, increasingly panoramic view opens up. At a junction in 1.8km bear left with the salient path. Ignore ways off, and eventually the path ends at a track (700 metres). Here turn right, briefly following the Worsley Trail. Turn right at a road, and on the brow of a hill, by bus stops, turn left up Berry Lane. In 300 metres turn left (G15) to climb back onto a ridge. Take a quick look around; the Back of the Wight coastline is to the west, Bembridge Down to the east, and there may be a glimpse of the Solent and mainland to the north. Quite a view!

Turn right and at a junction of paths continue on G15, still on the ridge. In 400 metres ignore a gate on the right, but in a further 600 metres, by a telegraph pole, bear right to descend through a field. Turn right onto a lane and, in 150 metres, left on G19. Keep to your current direction and cross an infant **River Medina;** bear half-right after the footbridge to cross the field gate ahead. Keep to the right edge of this new field, and exit at the far side to turn right along a pleasant track, eventually emerging in the village of **Rookley** (pub), once an important brick-making and gravel-quarrying centre. ▸

Bus stops are 100 metres to the right.

To continue, turn left on the road and in 100 metres right on A37 with a view towards Arreton Down. At a T-junction in 1.5km turn right, and go left at

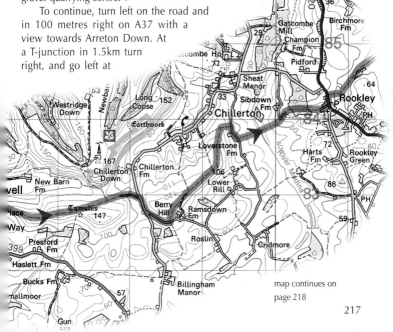

map continues on page 218

217

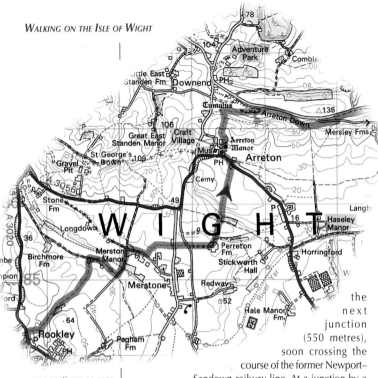

map continues on page 220

the next junction (550 metres), soon crossing the course of the former Newport–Sandown railway line. At a junction by a beautiful early 17th-century house (**Merston Manor**) turn right, and in 250 metres left on A1. If the path is unclear, bear half-right, shortly to exit the field onto a drive. Take the path opposite, through a gap in the hedge, to continue through three fields to a road and bus stops, the scenery slowly improving.

Cross the road and, shortly, a parallel lane to continue on a stony track. At **Perreton Farm** turn left through two gates in quick succession. Shortly after the second, turn sharp left up an escarpment to cross a stile. At a T-junction at the very end of the field, turn right, then, in 40 metres, go left downhill before steeply ascending the next escarpment and over another stile to the left. Continue towards the spread-out village of Arreton and the downland ridge of the walk's next stage.

Turn left at the road through **Arreton** (pub; Arreton Barns also has a pub and shops), close to bus stops. Then at the White Lion pub turn right up A12. Just past Arreton Church, turn left for a detour around Arreton Barns: a hotchpotch of olde-worlde shops and eateries, aimed squarely at tourists but no less charming for that. Back at the church, continue on the path signposted to **Arreton Down**, soon with a good view back towards the church and the southeast downs beyond.

Arreton Church was reconstructed in the 12th century (with later additions), but remains of the

Arreton Church

original Saxon church can still be seen, such as the faded wall-painting and narrow window in the north wall, and the middle window in the west wall.

Bear right past an information board towards the top of the down to ascend to, and continue along, its ridge beside a fence admiring the spectacular 180-degree view (the best yet) and the wonderful, bracing air.

Arreton Down is particularly noted for its Great Green Bush Cricket population, but also hosts a wide variety of birds (such as kestrel, buzzard and woodpecker) and flowers (up to 40 species per square metre, including vetches, scabious and harebells). Winter grazing keeps the less graceful vegetation at bay.

A gate will soon come into view, beyond power cables. Having crossed it, continue on a narrow path, still near the ridge just shy of the road. In about 700 metres the path becomes sandwiched between a lane and a hollow; the path soon enters the latter and shortly arrives at a wooden barrier, which is crossed to emerge onto the country lane. Turn left and in 70 metres sharp right on A16, almost immediately turning left to ascend to a path T-junction just shy of the main road. Turn right.

Just after the field on your right ends, go through

a gap in the hedgerow to cross the road and continue quarter-right on R16, over the pathless grass towards the plateau atop **Mersley Down**. Post holes recently discovered on the down's southern slope (beyond the road) are evidence of an iron-age vineyard. The panoramic view at the top is one of the best on the island.

Descend in the same direction, obliquely away from the road, and in a few hundred metres head towards a footpath signpost, increasingly visible. Turn right on the lane and in 90 metres take R17 half-right across the pathless grass towards a soon-visible signpost. Cross the road carefully to continue on NC2. Immediately bear right over a stile and, after admiring the expanse of woodland below, continue towards the wood straight ahead on a faint path, aiming for a stile visible below, just north of the hamlet of Knighton. ▶ Find and follow bridleway NC4 nearly opposite – a curiously atmospheric valley path – eventually ascending steeply to a T-junction. Here, turn left, and left again on a narrow path just before the road.

There is a bus stop 150 metres on the right.

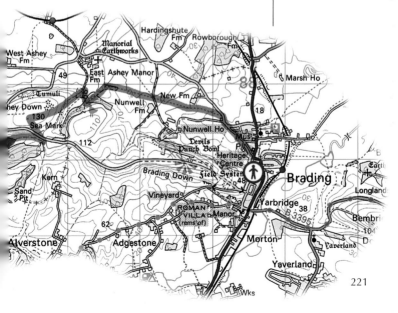

Ashey Sea Mark

In 100 metres cross the road and ascend the field, quarter-left, to the Sea Mark on top of **Ashey Down** and another exquisite view.

> The **Sea Mark** was erected in 1735 to convey semaphore signals to Portsmouth in respect of maritime craft in the island's waters. It can be seen when crossing the Solent from Portsmouth.

Head east towards the bushes, then in about 300 metres, or 70 metres before a hillock ahead, bear half-right on a just-discernible path obliquely towards a belt of woodland in the valley below. Soon the path becomes more prominent, and at the edge of the plateau take a combination of paths which descend to the valley floor. When there, continue past two troughs to find a stile tucked away near the far right corner of the woodland ahead. Keep a brick wall on your left to follow B34 and, at the next junction, turn left on B24. In 300 metres bear left to enter more woodland, then immediately bear right.

Once back in the open, go through a gap in the hedgerow ahead to walk through a vast field. Stay in your

Nunwell House

current direction through three more fields. At the top of the giant fourth field, head towards a fence just visible ahead on the left, soon noticing Nunwell House to the right, in the shadow of **Brading Down** (see Walk 30). Pass to the right of the farm that the fence encloses, with the village of Brading – your destination – soon visible. Yet another lovely setting.

Continue through a fifth and final field heading towards the village. On reaching a road turn right with care, passing the entrance to **Nunwell House** and bearing right into Doctors Lane a little further ahead. At the road junction inside **Brading** (pubs, restaurant/café, fish and chip shop, grocery store, toilets), continue down West Street to reach the Town Hall and the bus stops. For Brading Station, follow the road around the bend and take Station Road on the left.

WALK 33
Godshill to Ventnor

Start	The Griffin pub, Godshill
Finish	Ventnor
Distance	8.6km (5.4 miles)
Grade	Moderate
Time	2½hr
Refreshments	None en route
Public transport	To start: bus routes 2 and 3; from finish: bus routes 3 and 6
Parking	Car park opposite The Griffin pub
Early finish	South of Wroxall (6.2km, bus route 3)

This is a particularly beautiful downland walk, perfect for a sunny day. Little-used permissive paths starting just south of Godshill ascend to the transmitter on top of Appuldurcombe Down, which provides a sensational view. After following the ridge of Stenbury Down and descending to the Wroxall valley, there is a steep ascent of Wroxall Down, with a tranquil sea opening up around. A magnificent view of Ventnor from up on high is one of the highlights of the walk.

Walk up Hollow Lane next to The Griffin in **Godshill** (pubs, cafés, shops, toilets), turning left almost immediately onto footpath GL57. Beyond a swing gate at the start of a wood (550 metres), ignore paths on the left and right to maintain the current direction. Stay on the main path through the wood, turn right at a T-junction (250 metres) and left at another a short distance later. Go over a stile, and in 400 metres, with field gates on your left and right, take the main fork half-right to continue uphill towards trees. Then, at a major junction after 400 metres, ignore the first path on the right (GL49), and instead take the track to the right of the two paths ahead (a permissive footpath).

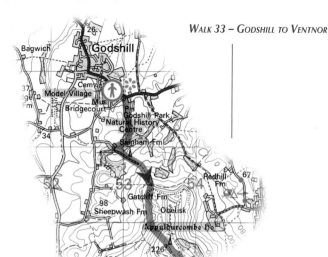

map continues on
page 226

In 550 metres turn right through a gate (now with a southwesterly vista) and in 100 metres turn left on a faint grassy path, keeping gorse bushes on your left. Then, at the top of the current incline, turn right on a wide, grassy

*Northeasterly view
from permissive path
ascending the downs*

path, ascending gradually, with the view ever more comprehensive. Go through a gate (450 metres) and bear left towards the radio transmitter on top of **Appuldurcombe Down** for an incredible panoramic view. Look to the southeast to spot Whitwell, and Niton beyond.

Head along the track leading from the transmitter to pass a second transmitter further along the ridge, now on **Stenbury Down**. Spot the Ventnor suburb of Lowtherville ahead to your left. Ignore all descents from the ridge; but, 950 metres from the second transmitter, look out for, and cross, a stile on the left, descending initially through a golf course. Follow the yellow arrows; a track beside field gates is reached in 650 metres, after which bear slightly right towards another post with a yellow arrow. Having descended to a lane running through the valley, turn left and follow the stone wall to continue on V13, which climbs to the main road by bus stops. Cross to continue on V13 opposite, ignoring ways off. The sea soon becomes visible – a picture of serenity.

The path leads onto Wroxall Down, now with panoramic views. But the best is yet to come. Bear right off the main path just beyond a bench and signpost, initially in the

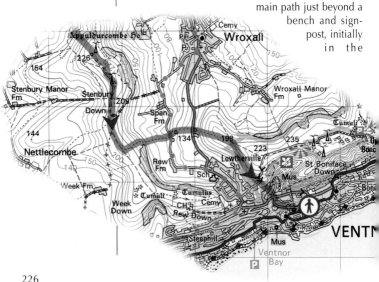

direction of the sea. Ignore path offshoots. On almost reaching a lane on the left (550 metres) walk clockwise round the field ahead (ignore the path between hedge-rows), soon to cross a stile on the left leading onto the lane. Turn left and immediately right to find one of the most magnificent views on this side of the island: Ventnor spread out at your feet, with miles of sea to the southeast beyond.

Descend the very steep path (soon stepped), and turn right at the bottom to reach a road. ▶ For the centre of **Ventnor** (accommodation, supermarkets, pubs, cafés, restaurants, shops, toilets), take the sloping path opposite and first right (Tulse Hill) to emerge at the bus stop in High Street.

You may wish to detour into the adjacent industrial estate, formerly Ventnor Station. Steam trains from Ryde used to use the tunnel still visible at the far end.

APPENDIX A
Route summary table

Walk number	Walk title	Distance	Time	Grade	Refreshments en route?	Early finish option?	Page
Coastal Path (south coast)							
1	Sandown to Ventnor	10.5km (6.6 miles)	2½hr	Easy–moderate	Yes	Yes	39
2	Ventnor to Chale	12.3km (7.7 miles)	3½hr	Moderate	Yes	Yes	44
3	Chale to Brook	13.2km (8.3 miles)	3hr	Mainly easy	Yes	Yes	49
4	Brook to Alum Bay	11.9km (7.4 miles)	3hr	Moderate	Yes	Yes	53
Coastal Path (north coast)							
5	Alum Bay to Yarmouth	8.7km (5.4 miles)	2½hr	Fairly easy	Yes	Yes	59
6	Yarmouth to Shalfleet	12.7km (7.9 miles)	3hr	Easy	No	No	63
7	Shalfleet to East Cowes	16.7km (10.4 miles)	4hr	Easy	Yes	No	67

Walk number	Walk title	Distance	Time	Grade	Refreshments en route?	Early finish option?	Page
8	East Cowes to Ryde	12.7km (7.9 miles)	3hr	Fairly easy	Yes	Yes	72
9	Ryde to Sandown	19.1km (11.9 miles)	5½hr	Fairly easy	Yes	Yes	78
West Wight							
10	Shorwell circular	16km (10 miles)	4hr	Moderate	No	Limited	88
11	Shorwell to Niton	14km (8.8 miles)	3½hr	Moderate	No	Yes	93
12	Brighstone circular	13.3km (8.3 miles)	3hr	Moderate	Yes*	Limited	99
13	Brighstone to Yarmouth	13.3km (8.3 miles)	3hr	Moderate	No	Yes	104
14	Best of eastern Freshwater (circular)	11.2km (7 miles)	2½hr	Easy	Yes	Yes	109
15	Best of western Freshwater (circular)	16.3km (10.2 miles)	4½hr	Moderate	Yes	Yes	115
16	Shalfleet and Newtown circular	11.4km (7.1 miles)	3hr	Easy	No	Yes	121

Walk number	Walk title	Distance	Time	Grade	Refreshments en route?	Early finish option?	Page
17	Shalfleet to Newport	22.2km (13.9 miles)	5½hr	Fairly easy	Yes	Yes	126
18	Gatcombe to Newport	10.4km (6.5 miles)	3hr	Moderate	No	Yes	133
19	Tennyson Trail	17.3km (10.8 miles)	4hr	Fairly easy	No	No	138
East Wight							
20	Shanklin circular via Nettlecombe	27.6km (17.3 miles)	7hr	Moderate	Very limited	Yes	144
21	Shanklin circular via Bonchurch	10.5km (6.6 miles)	2½hr	Moderate	Yes	Yes	153
22	Shanklin circular via America Wood	9.5km (5.9 miles)	2½hr	Moderate	No	Yes	158
23	Shanklin to Godshill	7.4km (4.6 miles)	2hr	Fairly easy	No	Yes	162
24	Niton circular (the two lighthouses walk)	14.5km (9.1 miles)	4hr	Moderate	Yes	Yes	165

Walk number	Walk title	Distance	Time	Grade	Refreshments en route?	Early finish option?	Page
25	Ashey Station circular	15km (9.4 miles)	3½hr	Moderate	Very limited	Limited	170
26	Ryde to Ventnor	29.3km (18.3 miles)	7½hr	Easy–strenuous	Yes	Yes	175
27	Seaview circular	19.9km (12.4 miles)	5hr	Moderate	Yes	Yes	184
28	Wootton Bridge circular	17.9km (11.2 miles)	4½hr	Fairly easy	Yes	Limited	191
29	Wootton Bridge to Newport	10.3km (6.4 miles)	2½hr	Easy	Yes	Yes	196
30	Bembridge Trail	20.1km (12.6 miles)	5½hr	Fairly easy–moderate	Yes	Yes	201
31	Worsley Trail	21.7km (13.6 miles)	5½hr	Moderate	Yes	Yes	209
32	Shorwell to Brading	22.4km (14 miles)	6½hr	Moderate	Yes	Yes	216
33	Godshill to Ventnor	8.6km (5.4 miles)	2½hr	Moderate	No	Yes	224

*Tearoom inside attraction (admission fee)

APPENDIX B
Useful contacts

Tourist information
The official tourist website www.islandbreaks.co.uk has a wealth of up-to-date information including current events, accommodation and where to eat. The tourism telephone service can be reached on 01983 813813.

At the time of writing, there are 15 Tourist Information Points throughout the island, located in all the towns, resorts, and even popular villages such as Godshill and Brighstone. You can check locations and opening times at www.visitisleofwight.co.uk/travel/tourist-information-points.

For more detailed information, look at the weekly Isle of Wight County Press (www.iwcp.co.uk), and do check out Matt and Cat's frank and witty personal reviews of the island's eateries at www.mattandcat.co.uk/reviews.

Transport
Ferries
Wightlink
www.wightlink.co.uk
Tel: 0333 999 7333
email via website

Red Funnel
www.redfunnel.co.uk
Tel: 0844 844 9988
post@redfunnel.co.uk

Hovercraft
Hovertravel
www.hovertravel.co.uk
Tel: 01983 717700
info@hovertravel.com

Buses
Southern Vectis
www.islandbuses.info
Tel: 01983 827000
talk2us@southernvectis.com
(See 'Getting around' in the Introduction for an indication of daily frequency)

Train
Island Line
www.southwesttrains.co.uk
Tel: 01983 812591
email via website

Parking
For car park locations and charges search
www.iwight.com

Tide times
Search the Isle of Wight County Press website
www.iwcp.co.uk

Libraries (including internet access)
Search
www.iwight.com

Island societies
Isle of Wight Natural History and Archaeological Society
www.iwnhas.org

Hampshire & Isle of Wight Wildlife Trust
www.hiwwt.org.uk

Biodiversity www.wildonwight.co.uk

NOTES

NOTES

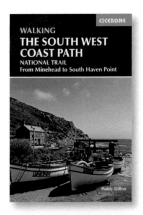

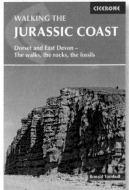
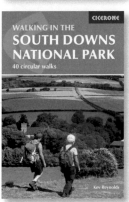

The Great Outdoors

DIGITAL EDITIONS

30-DAY
FREE TRIAL

- Substantial savings on the newsstand price and print subscriptions
- Instant access wherever you are, even if you are offline
- Back issues at your fingertips

Downloading **The Great Outdoors** to your digital device is easy, just follow the steps below:

1 **Download the App** from the App Store

2 **Open the App**, click on 'subscriptions' and choose an annual subscription

3 **Download** the latest issue and enjoy

Available on the **App Store**

The digital edition is also available on

The 30-day free trial is not available on Android or Pocketmags and is only available to new subscribers

 Available on Android

 **pocket**mags.com

LISTING OF CICERONE GUIDES

Walking – Trekking – Mountaineering – Climbing – Cycling

Over 40 years, Cicerone have built up an outstanding collection of over 300 guides, inspiring all sorts of amazing adventures.

 Every guide comes from extensive exploration and research by our expert authors, all with a passion for their subjects. They are frequently praised, endorsed and used by clubs, instructors and outdoor organisations.

All our titles can now be bought as **e-books**, **ePubs** and **Kindle** files and we also have an online magazine – **Cicerone Extra** – with features to help cyclists, climbers, walkers and trekkers choose their next adventure, at home or abroad.

Our website shows any **new information** we've had in since a book was published. Please do let us know if you find anything has changed, so that we can publish the latest details. On our **website** you'll also find great ideas and lots of detailed information about what's inside every guide and you can buy **individual routes** from many of them online.

It's easy to keep in touch with what's going on at Cicerone by getting our monthly **free e-newsletter**, which is full of offers, competitions, up-to-date information and topical articles. You can subscribe on our home page and also follow us on **Facebook** and **Twitter** or dip into our **blog**.

Cicerone – the very best guides for exploring the world.

CICERONE

2 Police Square Milnthorpe Cumbria LA7 7PY
Tel: 015395 62069 info@cicerone.co.uk
www.cicerone.co.uk and www.cicerone-extra.com

For full information on all our
guides, books and eBooks,
visit our website:
www.cicerone.co.uk